Proper Attitudes
Toward Leadership

by
Robyn Gool

Christian Publishing Services, Inc.
Tulsa, Oklahoma

Unless otherwise indicated, all Scripture quotations are taken from the *King James Version* of the Bible.

Proper Attitudes Toward Leadership
ISBN 0-88144-073-6
Copyright © 1987 by Robyn Gool
4401 Montibello Drive
Charlotte, N.C. 28226

Published by CHRISTIAN PUBLISHING SERVICES, INC.
P.O. Box 55388
Tulsa, Oklahoma 74155

Contents

Introduction

A great deal has been said and written recently in the media about Christian leaders. As a result, the Spirit of God has spoken to me that the Body of Christ must come to understand the role and nature of Christian leadership and what their attitudes should be toward these God-ordained leaders.

The Lord has impressed upon me that the Body of Christ must not allow itself to become conformed to the world. You and I must develop and maintain a proper attitude toward those who are set in positions of spiritual leadership over us. Our attitudes toward these people must be correct.

Attitudes are vitally important; they can cause us to win or to lose. Our attitude toward the Word of God must be right. Out attitude toward our brothers and sisters in Christ must also be right. Finally, our attitude toward the ministry gifts must be right. If they are not, we are in for trouble.

Many people have lost their jobs, not because they could not do the work assigned to them, but simply because their attitude was wrong. Because of their wrong attitude, they were always causing problems, creating turmoil, stirring up strife, and making everyone's job more difficult. That's why attitudes are so very important. No one can expect to succeed in life with a wrong attitude — especially toward those in positions of authority over him.

As I share with you in these pages concerning proper attitudes toward leadership, I would like for you to understand that I am specifically referring to leader-

5

ship in the Church of Jesus Christ. I am writing from the perspective of the Bible to see what it has to say concerning ministry gifts and the attitude members of the Body of Christ should have toward those God-given gifts.

Attitudes affect success in the spiritual realm just as they affect success in the natural realm. As you read, please remember this vital truth: your attitude determines your altitude.

1
Touch Not Mine Anointed

Wherefore he saith, When he ascended up on high, he led captivity captive, and gave gifts unto men.

(Now that he ascended, what is it but that he also descended first into the lower parts of the earth?

He that descended is the same also that ascended up far above all heavens, that he might fill all things.)

And he gave some, apostles; and some, prophets; and some, evangelists; and some, pastors and teachers.

Ephesians 4:8-11

Who is **he** to whom this passage is referring? Jesus Christ. According to the Apostle Paul, Jesus gave His Church gifts — apostles, prophets, evangelists, pastors and teachers. He established offices in His Church and He is still calling men and women to fill those offices today. Therefore, these are ministry *gifts* from the Lord Himself to His Church for our benefit and instruction.

For the perfecting of the saints, for the work of the ministry, for the edifying of the body of Christ.

Ephesians 4:12

In this verse we see that these ministry gifts were set in the Church for the perfecting of the saints, to do the work of the ministry — Christ's ministry. These offices have been established and filled with godly men and women for the purpose of maturing or developing the saints so that the saints will be able to do the work of the ministry and have a part themselves in the edifying or building up of the Church.

Those who fill these positions or offices are given to the Church by Jesus Christ. Therefore, they are gifts to the Church. That is the first thing that we must recognize about these people, that they are gifts to us from the Lord and should be treated as such.

You will notice that I said "men *and* women." Some people, even some men of God, have trouble with women being in the ministry. I don't have any trouble with that because God doesn't have any problem with it. The Bible states that in Jesus Christ there is neither male nor female. (Gal. 3:28.) God Himself declares that in the last days He will pour out His Spirit upon all flesh and that His sons *and His daughters* will prophesy. (Joel 2:28.) Besides that, we know that God has used women throughout the Bible to carry His message and accomplish His will. Who will dare say that He cannot do that today?

Now some say that the Apostle Paul was a male chauvinist because of some of his stated views on the role of women in the Church. But that is not true. If you study the Scriptures correctly, you will see that Paul commended women in the ministry.

So I have no problem with women in the ministry. Neither should you. The people whom the Lord has set in the Body as ministry gifts must be received as from Him. That is the first attitude you and I ought to have. The apostle, the prophet, the evangelist, the pastor and teacher are from God. Each (whether male or female) is a gift from God.

Today, sad to say, some ministers of the Gospel have come under attack in the media. Worse than that, even some Christians have joined in that attack. That's why the Body of Christ must be taught in the area of proper attitudes toward leadership.

These men and women are called into these offices by God. As such, they need to be treated with respect.

One man had the gall to write in an article: "Watch out. Oral Roberts is saying he's heard from God again; he's talking about a cure for cancer. Guard your pocketbook!"

Many Christians have also talked improperly or wrongly about the men and women of God. That must stop! We may not agree wholeheartedly with everything that is being said or done by ministers of the Gospel, but we must not put ourselves in the position of judging them. Our attitude must be, "I may not always understand or agree with these people, but they are my brothers and sisters in Christ and I will not criticize them!" We need to learn to weep with those who weep, and rejoice with those who rejoice; to bear one another's burdens and so fulfill the law of Christ.

We must have the proper attitude toward leadership in the Body of Christ. Notice that it was Jesus Who gave some as apostles, some as prophets, some to be evangelists, and some to serve as pastors and teachers. He gave them to us for our benefit and welfare. That means that your pastor is a pastor to the Body of Christ. Oral Roberts is an evangelist to the Body of Christ. Kenneth Copeland is a prophet and teacher to the Body. We must bear in mind that the ministry gifts are for the Body — the whole Body. It's not, "I am of Apollos, I am of Cephas, I am of Paul" — no, all things (including these ministry gifts) are ours! They're gifts from God to the whole Body.

As I continue with this subject, it may seem that I am talking primarily about the pastor, but I would like for you to keep in mind that I'm speaking about all the ministry gifts. It will be easier to teach by referring to the pastoral gift or office, but I am in no way teaching this because of some problem in my own church or in an attempt to build up my own position. I am teaching it simply because I believe it is a subject that needs to be brought to the attention of all Christians everywhere, regardless of their church situation or affiliation. This is a message which is needed at this moment. It's time for us Christians to link arms and to walk together in love and harmony. It's time we learned to bless, to exhort, to comfort, to edify one another! We need to join hands and pull together. Let's let the world see that we are one! Whether we are black or white, red or yellow, male or female, denominational or independent, let's show the world that we are one in Christ, in Whom there is no division by color, gender, race or label.

Twice in the Bible, the Lord makes this bold statement: **. . . Touch not mine anointed, and do my prophets no harm** (1 Chron. 16:22; Ps. 105:15). Even though the entire nation of Israel is referred to as God's anointed, there is a distinction made between them and the leadership, the prophets. Those whom Jesus Christ has set in the Church as apostles, prophets, evangelists, pastors or teachers make up the distinction today. They ought not to be "touched" adversely. To do so is to stand on dangerous ground. God warned against harming His ministers, and we would do well to heed that warning. The Lord doesn't waste His breath saying things He doesn't mean. He says what He means, and He means what He says. Many people today are sick and others have died prematurely simply because they have dared to "touch" the men and women of God. They have criticized them, persecuted them, maligned them, ridiculed them, when God has clearly said not to touch them or to do them harm.

People who talk about men like Jim Bakker or Oral Roberts or any other man or woman of God are treading on thin ice. You and I ought to make sure we are not out on that thin ice with them. It's time we developed the right attitude toward those whom God has set in positions of authority and responsibility. We may not understand or agree with everything they say or do, but we do need to learn to keep our mouths shut about it. It would do well for us to learn not to spend our lunch break criticizing some minister or ministry. Certainly we ought never to engage in negative conversations with unbelievers about these men and women whom God has chosen and ordained. How can unbelievers understand anything about spiritual matters? Unless they are born again they can't understand anything about God's anointing or about spiritual things. The Bible says that such things are only spiritually discerned. We must learn not to touch God's anointed nor to harm His prophets — even with our mouths!

I believe that for every one of us who has talked wrongly or adversely about a man or woman of God and their ministry, this ought to be a day of repentance. This day we should confess before God, "Father, forgive me, I know not what I do."

The Body of Christ ought to be doing what the Apostle Paul recommends in Ephesians 4:3: **Endeavoring to keep the unity of the Spirit in the bond of peace.** We may not agree when the rapture is going to take place — pre-tribulation, mid-tribulation, or post-tribulation — but we can all agree that Jesus is Lord!

We may not agree on speaking in tongues, but we can agree that Jesus is Lord! We may not agree on healing, or whether it is God's will to heal everyone, but we can agree on Who is Lord of all — Jesus! And since He is Lord, let's do as He prayed the Father we would do, and that is become one. Let's endeavor to keep unity in the Church.

Let's not mock and persecute each other, talk about one another and "bad mouth" one another. Let's not talk about Oral Roberts until we have gotten as many people saved as he has. Let's not talk about Jim Bakker until our Gospel television program is being broadcast around the world. Let's not condemn some other Christian or group for dancing before the Lord until we have done it ourselves and been told by God Himself that it displeases Him. Let's keep unity and a proper attitude toward our brothers and sisters in Christ, especially those in positions of leadership.

In verse 1 of Ephesians 4, Paul exhorts us, **I therefore . . . beseech you that ye walk worthy of the vocation wherewith ye are called.** Let's walk worthy of our vocation, our calling. We've been called to be Christ-like. We've been called to be Christ's ambassadors. We've been called to let all men everywhere see that we are His disciples by our love for each other. Let's walk worthy of that high calling.

Do you remember what the Lord said? He said not to touch His anointed ones and to do His prophets no harm. Any time we talk spitefully about God's ministry gifts, we are "touching" them and doing them harm. We expect outsiders to do that, they don't know any better. However, we expect more sense than that from other believers.

The other day I saw a letter to the editor of a newspaper, supposedly from a Christian. It read: "Thank you for exposing Jim Bakker. I'm a child of God, and now I'm going to speak out against that ministry every chance I get." Shame on that person. Even if I did feel that way, as a believer I wouldn't let the world know it. That's all they need, to have us Christians joining them in accusing and attacking our own brothers and sisters in the faith.

There are several reasons why we should have the proper attitude toward our Christian leaders.

Number one, *they are gifts from God to the Church.* Now, I understand that not everybody who claims to be a minister is really God-ordained. But we don't have to worry about exposing or opposing them. Jesus said that we will know false prophets by their fruits. He states that a good tree will bring forth good fruit, and a bad tree will bring forth bad fruit. Let's not waste time and effort worrying and fretting about the bad "trees," let's just take time to observe the fruit they are producing. It will soon become evident to all whether they are really of God or not.

Yes, I know there are wolves in sheep's clothing out there. But if you are a born-again, Spirit-filled, Spirit-led believer, that means that you hear your Shepherd's voice. If you are not sure whether your leader is a wolf or a sheep, the Lord will tell you quite clearly. He'll warn you to get away from the wolf if you need to!

Now if you are not sure that you know your Shepherd's voice, then that's another thing all together. But as for me, I know my Shepherd's voice, and a stranger I will not follow. So I don't have to be concerned with false prophets. Neither do you. Our Shepherd will warn us if we are following a wolf in sheep's clothing. We just need to spend time before the Lord. He'll tell us whether our leader is from Him or not. We don't have to be concerned with whether he or she has credentials from some church board or is affiliated with a particular denomination. We just go to the Shepherd and let Him inform us whether or not the person has been chosen, anointed, ordained and sent by Him. If he or she is God's anointed, His prophet, then we need to honor that person, whether we like or agree with them or not.

> **And it came to pass, when Saul was returned from following the Philistines, that it was told him, saying, Behold, David is in the wilderness of Engedi.**
>
> **Then Saul took three thousand chosen men out of all Israel, and went to seek David and his men upon the rocks of the wild goats.**
>
> **1 Samuel 24:1,2**

Saul was after David to kill him. The reason Saul was out to kill David was because he was jealous of him. Why would King Saul be jealous of David? Because he had received more praise from the people than Saul had.

Jealousy is nothing new. Many people are jealous of the men and women of God, that's why they talk against them so much. They are jealous because God is using others more than He is them. It is a shame to be jealous of another person for any reason, but especially because of his or her ministry. After all, we are all on the same team, fighting the same devil. Why should any of us be jealous of another person's ministry? If each of us will just do what the Lord calls us to do, we will be blessed, just as that man of God will be blessed if he is faithful and obedient. But when any of us tries to keep up with or surpass another minister, we just cause trouble for ourselves and bring shame on the cause of Christ.

So Saul was after David to kill him because of the spirit of malice, jealousy and envy that had come on him when he heard the women singing of how King Saul had slain his thousands but David his ten thousands. (1 Sam. 18:7.) Did you know that malice, jealousy and envy will kill you? If you have that spirit in your heart, you may wonder why you're hurting, why you're sick in your mind or body and why your medication or treatment doesn't help. You can't be well in mind or body for very long if you are sick in spirit. Sooner or later that unclean spirit in you will destroy you, one way or another. That's what it was doing to King Saul, driving him to self-destruction, though he thought it was David who was about to be destroyed.

> And he came to the sheepcotes by the way, where was a cave; and Saul went in to cover his feet: and David and his men remained in the sides of the cave.
>
> And the men of David said unto him, Behold the day of which the Lord said unto thee, Behold, I will deliver thine enemy into thine hand, that thou mayest do to him as it shall seem good unto thee. Then David arose, and cut off the skirt of Saul's robe privily.
>
> And it came to pass afterward, that David's heart smote him, because he had cut off Saul's skirt.
>
> **1 Samuel 24:3-5**

Now the picture is this: Saul has chosen 3,000 men to track down and kill David. He has heard that David is in a certain area where there are many caves. When Saul and his men arrive in that vicinity, he goes into one of the caves to "cover his feet." (That simply means that Saul went in a cave to relieve himself. In modern English, we would say that Saul went into a cave to go to the bathroom.)

It just so happened that, unknown to Saul, he had picked the very cave in which David and his men were hiding out from him. When David's men saw King Saul all alone, they urged David to take advantage of the situation. "David, this is the day the Lord told you about," they said to him. "This is the day He said would come when He would deliver your enemy into your hands to do with as you will. This is your day, David; go get him!"

Immediately, on impulse, he got up, took his sword in hand, sneaked in behind Saul, and cut the fringe off his garment. As we see in verse five, later on David was sorry for what he had done to Saul. Why? What was wrong with what David had done?

We must remember that originally God had hand-picked and anointed Saul to be king of Israel and to lead His people. But just because a person is chosen and anointed doesn't mean that he is always right in everything he says and does. Several times Saul was definitely wrong. Although it seemed that he deserved to be wiped out and removed from the throne because of his mistakes and wrong attitudes, David knew that he had no right to criticize or to pass judgment on God's anointed. If Saul needed to be removed from office, that was the job of the One Who had placed him in that office — it wasn't David's job.

Although it was wrong for Saul to be on David's trail to kill him, David still recognized Saul's calling and anointing. He knew it was wrong of him to touch or to harm God's anointed, even if he was in the wrong.

Sometimes we think that we are justified to do what we do because we know that the man or woman of God is wrong. But as the old saying goes, "Two wrongs don't make a right." For us to take matters into our hands and to execute judgment in God's place is doubly wrong. We must respect that authority, that calling, that position, that office — even if the person himself is wrong. Because when we fight against God's anointed, we are fighting against the Lord's gifts to His Church and against the Lord Himself.

Now do you see why I said that this should be a day of repentance? Because we've all done that. We've all set ourselves at some time, even if in ignorance, against God's anointed. We have talked wrongly about them. Some have even taken action against them. However, we must respect the authority, the calling, the office, the position of God's anointed servants. That's what David did.

Just because a person is called to be pastor of a church does not mean that he will always be right. He is a man like you and me. He just has to do his best. Even when he makes mistakes (and who doesn't?), he is still God's chosen and we need to recognize and respect that fact. It is not our right or place to take it upon ourselves to criticize, demean, oppose or "kick out" — get rid of — God's chosen servant. We must not touch him or harm him.

So the first attitude that you and I must have toward God's ministry gifts is to receive them as being from God, therefore, repecting them and their God-given position. They are given to us by the Lord Jesus.

One reason a lot of Christians are not in church on Sundays and other days of worship is because they haven't received the minister as being from God. Mark 6:30-35 states:

> And the apostles gathered themselves together unto Jesus, and told him all things, both what they had done, and what they had taught.
>
> And he said unto them, Come ye yourselves apart into a desert place and rest a while: for there were many coming and going, and they had no leisure so much as to eat.
>
> And they departed into a desert place by ship privately.
>
> And the people saw them departing, and many *knew him,* and *ran* afoot thither out of all cities, and *outwent* them, and came together unto him.
>
> And Jesus, when he came out, saw much people, and was moved with compassion toward them, because they were as sheep not having a shepherd: and he began to teach them many things.
>
> And when the day was now far spent, his disciples came unto him, and said, This is a desert place, and now the time is far passed.

Do you see it? Jesus was endeavoring to give His apostles some rest when suddenly He was recognized by the people. And the Bible states they ran afoot and came together unto Him. They recognized Jesus as the prophet of God, the anointed of God, the teacher of God — a gift from God! Nothing was going to keep them from receiving from Him. And they stayed all day, not considering their own bodies. That attitude produced a miracle.

I firmly believe that when the Body of Christ receives the ministry gifts, especially the pastor, as being from God, churches will be packed out and overflow. People won't want to sit home because they will know that the man or woman in charge of the service is God's gift to them. There will be an expectation, an anticipation, faith. They'll outrun the man or woman of God to the church, ready to receive, and they won't be concerned about time. "Sleeping in" on Sundays will be a thing of the past. Staying home on Sunday evenings and other days of worship will fade away. The gift will be recognized! Miracles will flow!

2
Are You in the Right Church?

If we are a part of a fellowship, ministry, or church with which we cannot agree, then we ought to ask ourselves whether it was God Who placed us there or whether it was our own decision. If we know that God has led us to the church or fellowship, then we can receive the minister as a gift from God and take on the attitude of being a blessing, and not "rocking the boat." There are too many believers in churches causing problems because they're in the wrong place.

We are all set in the Church to be part of the answer and not part of the problem. We are supposed to have the right attitude toward the ministry we are called to be involved in, catch hold of the God-given vision, and to "hook into" that vision so we can do our part in accomplishing the will of God.

So the next question after realizing these are gifts from God and God has given them their assignment is "Am I where I'm supposed to be?"

If you cannot receive your leader as being from God, then you are obviously in the wrong place. You need to get out now before you cause any more harm, because if you feel your leader is wrong, then sooner or later you will begin to criticize, find fault, lay blame, ridicule, and stir up strife. Eventually you will gather a little clique around you of others who agree with you against the leadership. But if that leadership is of God, then it will become evident that God is displeased with your behavior.

The problem could be that you are simply in the wrong place. If you are in the proper place, then your attitude ought to reflect it. Your attitude should be as right as your position. There's blessing in being in the right place. Abraham's ram was on a specific mountain. Elijah's water and food were at a certain brook. When the brook dried up, the widow who was to feed him was in a certain city. There is a perfect place for you. Your growth is there, your healing is there, your blessings are there.

Many times people find themselves unhappy and cause trouble simply because they are not where they should be. A lot of folks are simply in the wrong church.

Some people are in churches that never get along with their leader, whoever he is. Those churches are made up of people who like to complain and find fault. No matter what the leader says or does, they are going to criticize him, talk about him behind his back, tear down with their mouths everything he tries to build with his hands. Every Sunday after services, instead of roast beef for Sunday dinner, they have "roast preacher." They sit around the dinner table and "roast" their pastor with the words of their mouths.

If that's the way your church is, then you're not in the place God really wants you. You need to get out and find the place the Lord Jesus wants you to be in. The Lord wants you where you can receive the person in charge as being of God and from God. It's only when you can do that that you will ever benefit from the authority and anointing that comes with the office instituted by God.

There is a spiritual authority that accompanies every spiritual office. There is also an anointing placed by God that accompanies the office itself and will rest upon the person who fills that office — whoever he or she might be. When you are where God wants you to be, and you receive your spiritual leader as being from God, then you are in a position to begin to truly benefit from the authority and anointing upon that office and person. But if you are in the wrong place where people do not respect their leader, or especially if you are in the wrong because *you* do not respect your leader, then you have stepped out from under the authority and anointing that God has placed upon the person who fills that position of leadership. As a result, you won't benefit from being where you are, no matter how hard you work or how much you pray — or give.

You see, many people in churches are tithing, but they have a wrong attitude toward the pastor. They are wondering why they aren't being blessed in proportion to their giving. One reason is that they haven't received the man of God yet. You can tithe and tithe and give and give and give, but if your attitude toward the man of God is wrong, you can't benefit from the principles and concepts of God because you haven't received the gift He has given to the Church. If you *won't* receive God's ministry gifts, you *can't* receive His material gifts!

In order to benefit from God's material gifts and blessings, we must have the proper attitude toward His spiritual gifts. So it would be good for you and me to learn to respect and honor the man of God, if for no other reason than to make sure there is no hindrance to our receiving from the Lord.

So our first attitude should be, "Because I believe this person has been set in a position of spiritual authority by God Himself, I receive him (or her) as from the Lord." Our second attitude should be, "Since I receive this person as from the Lord and believe both of us are where we are supposed to be, then I will be and receive God's blessing. I won't 'rock the boat.' "

If you are not sure whether you are where you should be, then you need to pray and allow your Chief Shepherd to lead you to the fold in which you belong and where you can be and receive God's blessing. There is a fold for every person. Every individual believer ought to have a pastor. Despite what you may hear some people say, there is no such thing as a "television pastor."

Some Christians say, "Oh, I don't have to go to church; Fred Price (or Kenneth Copeland, or Oral Roberts, or some other media minister) is my pastor." That's just not so — not unless that person lives in the same area as that preacher and has joined that minister's local church. All of these men and women of God will tell you they are not on television to be your pastor. They have no intention of taking away from the local congregations; on the contrary, they're trying to build up local churches. They go on television mainly to reach those who can't or won't be reached by any other means. Their goal is to ultimately have these people in a strong local church. You and I should not be among those who refuse to become a part of a local body of believers.

Radio and television ministries are set up to reach the unchurched, not so much the churched. Every person who is born again should have a local pastor.

24

Regardless of what you may have heard, unless he or she is physically unable to attend services for some good reason, no true Christian can be content to just sit at home and "watch church" on a regular basis. God never intended for His worship services to be a "spectator sport." The Bible warns us about . . . **for-saking the assembling of ourselves together . . . .** (Heb. 10:25). As part of the flock of God, each of us is supposed to have a personal shepherd (pastor). Jesus, the Chief Shepherd, wants to lead each of us to the right under-shepherd.

If you don't know if you are where you are supposed to be, then pray and allow the Lord to lead you to the right place. Once you are there, take on the attitude of, "I know the Lord has led me here to be a blessing."

Consider this. There are several different eating establishments in your area. There's probably a McDonald's, a Burger Chef, a Hardee's or Wendy's, or some other hamburger chain. Doubtless there is a Kentucky Fried Chicken, and probably one or more competitors like Church's Fried Chicken. There may be hot dog and taco stands, seafood shops, and various other fastfood outlets, both national and local. Then there are more expensive restaurants for an evening of real sophisticated dining. Why are there so many eating places and such a variety of them? So you can pick and choose where you want to eat! If there was only one cafe or restaurant in town, you may or may not like their menu, cooking, prices or atmosphere.

What am I saying? Just as there is a variety of different eating establishments in any given area which cater to the different segments of society represented in that city, there is also a variety of churches from which to pick and choose. As many fine Christian churches and ministries as there are in this nation of ours, there is bound to be one within reach of your home that you can agree with and contribute to. If you will allow Him to do so, your Shepherd, the Head of the Church, will guide you to that local assembly where you can be blessed and be a blessing.

Once you have been led to a certain church and are an official member of it, make up your mind to comply with the rules and regulations you find set up in it. One thing President Roberts told the freshmen students when we arrived at Oral Roberts University was: "I want to say one thing to you very seriously. You *chose* to come to this school . . . and now that you are here, I'm expecting you to conform to, comply with, every regulation and guideline of this university. If at any time we see that you cannot conform to, comply with, the regulations and guidelines and principles of conduct of this university, we'll buy your bus ticket home."

What he was saying was: "If you can't conform to and comply with what you find here, then you need to go someplace else and not cause yourself or us problems." That's good advice when choosing a church. Find a place where you can be fed, where you can be blessed, where you can be a blessing and not a curse, where you can be part of the answer and not the problem. Find a church where you can "hook in" with the leader's calling and anointing and vision. Be a part of helping that vision to come to pass. Churches don't need people to rock the boat, they need people who will help keep the boat on course.

Once you've chosen your church (like choosing your restaurant), you may not always like the way things are done (the way the food is cooked up and served). But whether you like everything or not, make it a point to "hook in" with the leadership and go to work to make things better for everyone involved. If you can't operate in that situation, then find one in which you can operate. There is more than one church, ministry or outreach in your area.

If what is being served where you are now is not to your taste, then don't try to change the menu for everybody else, just go where you like what is being served. Ask the Lord to help you find where you will be happy and a help and an asset to those in charge. He'll do it. Keep in mind, however, that there will probably not be a place where everything is one hundred percent to your satisfaction all of the time. Nobody's perfect, not even you.

We need to remember that Jesus Himself has given the ministry gifts to His Church universal, and to the local church. They are given for our benefit. Remember also that we cannot benefit from those gifts if we have a wrong attitude.

A pastor is not *your* pastor unless you let him pastor you. You can have your name on the church roll, go through ten weeks of classes, shake the pastor's hand at the altar and become a member of that congregation, but until your attitude is such that you allow the pastor to exercise a pastoral influence upon you, he's not *your* pastor.

Over the years I've seen members of one church go to the pastor of another church for spiritual counsel and guidance, simply because they didn't receive the pastor as *their* pastor. If you do that, you are missing out on the spiritual authority and anointing that is on your pastor and his office, and you're making it hard for God to bless you. There is a calling that comes from God first, then there is an anointing and a spiritual authority that accompany that calling. Take advantage of it by letting the ministry gift set in your church pastor you.

Nobody is going to force you to go to a particular fellowship or church. It is strictly your choice. So wherever you choose to go, go there not only to be blessed but also to be a blessing. If you can't be a blessing where you are now, but are always causing strife and contention, then ask yourself seriously if you are really where you are supposed to be. Ask the Lord about your current situation. Follow His leadership and guidance. If He leads you out of that church, then go.

Many times people will say, "I'm not leaving this church. My grandmother went here, my mother went here, I was raised here, and I'm not leaving!" If that is your attitude, then you'd better leave. That attitude is wrong, and with a wrong attitude, sooner or later you will begin to cause trouble. At some point in time you will start to say, "I've been here a long time and I don't like the way this church is being run. I don't like this pastor. I don't agree with the way he does things. I've been a part of this church all my life and no outsider is going to come in here and start changing things around!"

Do you know what you are doing when you say things like that? You are touching God's anointed. You're harming the ministry gift. You are stepping over onto dangerous ground where the devil can come in to steal, kill, and destroy. Instead, you ought to follow your Shepherd and allow His will to be done.

Never try to force things. Don't take the attitude, "I'm gonna stay here and God's going to use me to change this place!" That's a lie! That shows spiritual immaturity. You're just a baby when you think that way. You obviously don't understand spiritual authority, call-ings, anointings, or the love walk. God is not going to use you to change a church or a pastor. The Lord has not called us to oppose spiritual authority, but to conform to it and comply with it. He's not called us to tear down, but to build up. We're not called to change others, but to change ourselves.

So, if that is your attitude, get it out of your head that God has called you to change His Church or any local branch of it. If the local church does need chang-ing, the Lord will begin with the ministry gift. He will deal directly with the heart of the pastor He has called and those set in the positions of authority and leader-ship. If there is a problem in the church leadership, the thing you and I should do is to pray and intercede for them. If the pastor is wrong, he needs our prayers, not our opposition, criticism, or condemnation. God can correct or change him.

If you sincerely feel that your pastor is wrong, then go and share your honest convictions with him personally and privately. If he cannot agree with you and says so, then leave that pastor and church and find one with whom you can agree. But don't leave negatively or with bitterness. We must walk in love.

Staying there and sharing your convictions about the pastor with other people in the congregation is touching God's anointed. You're doing a disservice to his position and the church because you're stirring up strife and disharmony. You may call yourself doing good when in reality you are doing great harm. When you cannot agree with a pastor or a church in major spiritual matters (not the color of the carpet), the best thing to do is to come out and be separate. Yet you should continue to pray, and to walk in love.

Some people will say, "Oh, I can't leave this church because God has put me here to pray for it." That's not so. You can pray for that church at home! If you and the pastor are in a spirit of disagreement and disharmony, then you won't be able to sit in services and receive from God and will probably be tempted to fuss and fume and "give an evil eye." Staying there to pray doesn't work.

Others make the mistake of going around and sharing everything they know and feel about the ministry gift with people they think will understand and sympathize. First of all, the Bible says that if you have anything against your brother, go to him and him alone. Secondly, you don't always know the people to whom you are sharing your innermost feelings, emotions, and convictions. They may get on the telephone and tell every bit of it to the person you least wanted to hear it. If you have something against the pastor and you share that information with a neighbor, he might go straight to the pastor with it.

There are those who stay in a church because they own a cemetery plot on the church grounds. That's no reason to stay in a dead church. Let the dead bury the dead. Go someplace where there is life. Besides, personally I don't plan on filling a grave plot. I plan on living right up until the time I am caught up in the

Rapture at the return of Jesus. How about you? I believe that this is the generation that will usher in the return of the Lord Jesus.

If you are caught in a dead church, a lifeless church, get out and go someplace where there is life. Find a place where you can learn about healing, so you don't have to be sick any more. I drive through cities sometime and it seems to me that some of the churches I see seem to have more people in their cemetery than they do in their sanctuary (judging by the size of the building). I always think to myself, "That pastor must not be teaching the Bible, if that many of his people are dying or dead!"

Jesus said that He came to earth that we might have life — life in all its fullness and abundance. (John 10:10.) The Bible tells us that by the stripes He bore on His back, we were healed. (Is. 53:5.) In the Old Testament, God said to His people, "I am the Lord that healeth thee." (Ex. 15:26.) Christians need to be in a church where these truths of life and health are taught. We need to be going to services in which there is life being ministered to the people.

Jesus said to His followers, "The words that I speak to you are spirit and life." (John 6:63.) He also said that man shall not live by bread alone, but by every word that proceeds from the mouth of God. (Matt. 4:4.) You ought not be satisfied with attending a church which preaches only salvation. Once a person gets saved, he doesn't need that message any more. He needs to move on into other areas. He needs to learn how to be healed and how to to walk in health. He needs to learn how to minister life and health to others by the laying on of hands. He needs to know about the casting out of demons, and the principles of faith. It's time for him to get more out of the Word of God than simply sitting week after week and being told over and over that Jesus saves!

In Matthew 5:29,30 our Lord tells us that if our eye offends us, we should pluck it out; or if our hand offends us, we should cut it off. Well, we should learn a lesson from those words. If a minister, a ministry or a ministry gift offends you, then you should "pluck it out," and "cut it off." If someone is preaching something that you know is not edifying and not in accordance with the Word of God, then get out from under his teaching. If he's preaching one thing and living another, then cut yourself off from him. Get away from there. Don't just go on week after week hoping that one day he'll see the light and change. Find yourself a place where the Gospel is being preached by those who also practice it.

This doesn't mean that you don't walk in love toward that person, ministry or church. It just means that you "cut them off" so you are no longer offended and led astray or into strife or turmoil or error.

If you do decide to stay in a church and have a hard time accepting what the pastor is teaching, at least respect his position, if not the person. When you go to church, even though you don't agree with everything he says, give him the respect due his office. God will bless that action. Either He'll work on the pastor to change him, or else He'll change you — inside or outside. He'll either alter your outlook and convictions or He'll lead you to another place of worship and service.

Many times staying in a particular church does more harm than good. When you become enlightened to the truth, you must walk in that truth. If you are a part of a dead church and you become enlightened to God's powerful Word and Spirit, then it would be better for you to change churches than it would be to go week after week to hear the same dull, dry, dead, unproductive sermons. When people ask you why you changed churches, you can let them know that, although you have nothing against the church or pastor, you moved on because you had found new life in Christ. You found out not only could you be saved by the blood of Jesus, but you can be healed, filled with the Spirit, prosper, cast out devils, and walk in authority. Praise God! That way, the report of your leaving (if handled properly and in love) can itself be a testimony to others that there is more light than what they are currently receiving. It may open doors for you to minister life to others in need of revival and renewal. Also, you can do it without causing strife within their church, because they came to you inquiring why you left.

There is another point about churches that I would like to make. You don't eat at McDonald's and pay at Wendy's. You pay where you are fed. If you are getting fed spiritually at a certain church, give there. If you are getting fed someplace else, don't keep on putting your money where there is no life. Many people are sitting in a pew week after week, putting their money into it a dead church that is really feeding no one. Tithe and give offerings where you're getting fed.

It's time we put away all these old ideas that have kept us bound to the past: "But this was my mama's church." "But I was raised in this church." "But this church is close to my house." "But I'm in the choir (or a deacon, or an usher, or a steward, or a Sunday School teacher)."

I understand past allegiances and I respect personal commitment. But the truth is, unless that church is truly feeding you and your family spiritually, then you need to find one that will. God is concerned about our spiritual well-being and growth. That's why He told us to seek first His kingdom and His righteousness. (Matt. 6:33.) He also tells us as newborn spiritual babes to desire the sincere milk of His Word so we may grow to be able to consume the real meat of the Word. (1 Pet. 2:2; 1 Cor. 3:2.) God is concerned about our growth. If we are in a place that is not growing and not contributing to our spiritual growth, then we need to seriously consider if the Lord is not calling us on to higher ground.

It's time for believers to get out of the realm of feelings and over into the realm of the Word and will of God. One will of His for every one of His children is that they grow into the likeness of His Son Jesus Christ. In order to do that, we need spiritual nourishment on a regular basis. If you aren't getting that where you now worship, then begin to ask the Lord what you should do about it.

Whatever decision the Lord lays on your heart, remember to keep a proper atitude toward those in spiritual authority. Remember that they are spiritual gifts from God the Father to His beloved children. Apostles, prophets, evangelists, pastors and teachers are to be received as gifts from God. Whoever these people are, whatever their Christian affiliation or background, if they are God's anointed then they should be received by the entire Body of Christ as His gifts.

We should never come against God's ministry gifts, doing them harm, not even with our mouths. God does not want those in the Body of Christ to persecute the ministry gifts.

If we can't agree with the spiritual leaders of our church, we should find another church in which we can operate in harmony and agreement. We should give our tithe and make our offerings to that church which feeds us spiritual food.

Finally, we should not become or remain attached to a dead church, one that does not hold forth the living Word of God in all its power and promise.

My wife once dated a young man who wasn't born again. She knew that the Bible warns against being unequally yoked with unbelievers, but she dated this man anyway. Every now and then the Spirit of the Lord would deal with her and tell her that she needed to drop her boyfriend because he would not give his heart to the Lord. Yet she kept on dating him, thinking she could change him.

Later on she found out that as long as she continued dating this young man, telling him he needed to change, he saw no need to change because it was obvious that she was accepting him as he was. She kept saying, "You need to change," and he kept thinking to himself, "I don't really need to change because she likes me the way I am, otherwise she wouldn't continue to go out with me."

That's the way it is with churches and church leaders. Sometimes they see no need to change their viewpoints and activities until they see themselves losing members to other churches. Then they wake up and begin to ask themselves what is happening or where they are failing their people. That's one reason I say it is better to leave a dead church than to remain in it hoping to change it from within. As long as you stay, you are giving the impression that you are in agreement with its lack of spirituality. On the other hand, your leaving may be just the spark needed to cause that pastor and church to begin to question their message, attitude and actions.

The Word of God declares: **Now I beseech you, brethren, by the name of our Lord Jesus Christ, that ye all speak the same thing, and that there be no divisions among you; but that ye be perfectly joined together in the same mind and in the same judgment** (1 Cor. 1:10).

It is the responsibility of every believer to get in a church and receive ministry where the ministry gift teaches and preaches what that person believes. It is your responsibility to be with like-minded people. That's a key to the elimination of strife.

If you're not sure that you're in the right church, or if you need direction concerning a church home, pray this prayer right now:

"Heavenly Father, I come to You in Jesus' name. I acknowledge Jesus as the Chief Shepherd of the sheep. Your Word says that Your sheep hear and know Your voice, and a stranger they will not follow. You will instruct us and teach us in the way that we should go. You will direct our paths. I receive Your Word now in Jesus' name.

"Heavenly Father, I ask You to show me if I'm in the right church, and lead me to the fellowship You want me to be in — to join. I desire spiritual growth; I desire maturity. I desire Your will for my life. I'll put aside all traps and traditions to follow You.

"Thank You for Your direction and for placing me where You want me. I believe that I receive right now — in Jesus' name. Amen."

3
God's Attitude

Moreover, brethren, I would not that ye should be ignorant, how that all our fathers were under the cloud, and all passed through the sea;

And were all baptized unto Moses in the cloud and in the sea;

And did all eat the same spiritual meat;

And did all drink the same spiritual drink: for they drank of that spiritual Rock that followed them: and that Rock was Christ.

But with many of them God was not well pleased: for they were overthrown in the wilderness.

1 Corinthians 10:1-5

Here the Apostle Paul is referring back to the nation of Israel, describing how they were all brought out of bondage by the Lord through the leadership of Moses. Although the people were all "baptized" in the Red Sea and although they all partook of the same spiritual food and drink, still God was not pleased with some of them, so they died in the wilderness. Why? What did they do to displease God?

In the following verses, Paul writes:

Now these things were our examples, to the intent we should not lust after evil things, as they also lusted . . . .

Neither murmur ye, as some of them also murmured, and were destroyed of the destroyer.

Now all these things happened unto them for ensamples: and they are written for our admonition . . . .

1 Corinthians 10:6,10,11

Paul tells us that these things happened to the children of Israel as examples for us today. God expects us to learn from the example of others who lived before us.

You see, contrary to what you may have heard, experience is not the best teacher. The Holy Spirit is the best Teacher. We can learn by reading the Bible and allowing the Holy Spirit of God to teach us by showing us what happened to different people in times past.

In verse 10 of this passage we see that these people murmured against their leaders and were destroyed because of it. They murmured against Moses time and time again.

"Moses, why did you bring us out here in this desolate place?" they would ask. "It was better for us back in Egypt."

They griped and complained and blamed Moses for all their troubles and unhappiness. They murmured against their God-ordained leadership so much and so long that finally God's anger was kindled to the point that He allowed destruction to come to some of them. God doesn't like for His people to come against His chosen, His anointed. God's ordained leaders might not always be right in their decisions and actions, but God has called them and placed them in the offices they occupy. It would do well for us to remember that fact.

> **And Miriam and Aaron spake against Moses because of the Ethiopian woman he had married: for he had married an Ethiopian woman.**
>
> **Numbers 12:1**

This raises an interesting question: Couldn't Moses marry whomever he wanted to marry? Did he have to have the approval of his brother Aaron and his sister Miriam before he could take a wife for himself? Yet Aaron and Miriam came against Moses because of the woman he married.

> And they said, Hath the Lord indeed spoken only by Moses? hath he not spoken also by us? And the Lord heard it.
>
> (Now the man Moses was very meek, above all the men which were upon the face of the earth.)
>
> And the Lord spake suddenly unto Moses, and unto Aaron, and unto Miriam, Come out ye three unto the tabernacle of the congregation. And they three came out.
>
> And the Lord came down in the pillar of the cloud, and stood in the door of the tabernacle, and called Aaron and Miriam: and they both came forth.
>
> And he said, Hear now my words: If there be a prophet among you, I the Lord will make myself known unto him in a vision, and will speak unto him in a dream.
>
> My servant Moses is not so, who is faithful in all mine house.
>
> With him will I speak mouth to mouth, even apparently, and not in dark speeches; and the similitude of the Lord shall he behold: wherefore then were ye not *afraid* to speak against my servant Moses?
>
> Numbers 12:2-8

Can you see God's attitude here toward those who come against His anointed?

You and I might not think that a man is anointed, but if he says he is called, then we had better not bother him. We might not be convinced that some of the pastors in our town are called of God, but if they have a church, then let's assume that God placed them there and leave them alone. If we can't go along with what they are saying and doing, let's at least leave them to the Lord to correct; after all, they are His servants, not ours. It is not a healthy practice to take it upon ourselves to straighten out the servants of the Almighty!

Notice verses 9 and 10:

> **And the anger of the Lord was kindled against them** (Aaron and Miriam); **and he departed.**
>
> **And the cloud departed from off the tabernacle; and, behold, Miriam became leprous, white as snow: and Aaron looked upon Miriam, and, behold, she was leprous.**

The anger of the Lord was kindled against Aaron and Miriam because they dared to come against His servant Moses. As a result of His anger, the Lord departed from their presence. When the presence of the Lord departed, Miriam instantly became leprous. Why? Because when she came against God's anointed, she came against God Himself.

To oppose God's anointed vessels is to oppose God Himself. To defy God's chosen, ordained leaders is to defy God. It is to say, "God, I don't agree with who You called into the ministry. I'm wiser than You and I think You made a bad choice. This person doesn't have the right to lead us."

Would any of us say to our Lord, "God, You made a mistake"? Yet when we murmur and complain, when we openly oppose God's anointed and His prophet, that's exactly what we are saying. Whenever we start persecuting the called of God, we are saying in essence, "God, I'm smarter than You. You messed up because You didn't consult with *me* before You made Your choice of leaders."

> And Aaron said unto Moses, Alas, my lord, I
> beseech thee, lay not the sin upon us, wherein we have
> done foolishly, and wherein we have sinned.
>
> Let her not be as one dead, of whom the flesh is
> half consumed when he cometh out of his mother's
> womb.
>
> And Moses cried unto the Lord, saying, Heal her
> now, O God, I beseech thee.
>
> Numbers 12:11-13

Notice what happens here. Seeing Miriam's hor-
rible condition, Aaron pleads with Moses not to punish
him and his sister for their foolishness and sinfulness
in speaking out against God's chosen leader. So Moses
pleads with God to heal Miriam and restore her to her
health. But look at the Lord's answer:

> And the Lord said unto Moses, If her father had
> but spit in her face, should she not be ashamed seven
> days? let her be shut out from the camp seven days,
> and after that let her be received in again.
>
> Numbers 12:14

In other words, God was saying, "No, Moses, I'm
not lettting this one go by that easily. If Miriam's earthly
father had just spit on her, she would be ceremonially
defiled and would have to spend seven days in purification. If she has the audacity to speak against My
anointed, then she is going to have to go through a
seven-day period of purification before I'll allow her
back into camp with the others."

What is God's message to us in this example from
the Old Testament? What is He telling us through this
story? *"Touch not mine anointed, and do my prophets no
harm."*

Now let's look back at Numbers 1:1:

> And when the people complained, it displeased
> the Lord: and the Lord heard it; and his anger was
> kindled; and the fire of the Lord burnst among them,
> and consumed them that were in the uttermost parts
> of the camp.

"And when the people complained, it displeased the Lord . . . ." That's the message I would like to burn into your consciousness through this book. God's anger is always kindled when we talk about or come against His leadership. God has not changed. In Malachi 3:6, He says, **. . . I am the Lord, I change not . . . .** Just because we are under grace doesn't mean that God's anger doesn't get kindled against us just as it did against these people who were under the law of Moses. No! God still detests for His Body to come against His anointed. He still has feelings.

". . . and the fire of the Lord burnst among them, and consumed them that were in the uttermost parts of the camp." If God did not spare those who murmured against His leaders back then, what makes us think He will spare us who murmer and complain today?

> And the people cried unto Moses; and when
> Moses prayed unto the Lord, the fire was quenched.
>
> And he called the name of the place Taberah:
> because the fire of the Lord burnst among them.
>
> Numbers 11:3,4

Notice what happens immediately after Moses had saved their very lives.

> And the mixt multitude that was among them fell
> a lusting: and the children of Israel also wept again,
> and said, Who shall give us flesh to eat?
>
> We remember the fish, which we did eat in Egypt
> freely; the cucumbers, and the melons, and the leeks,
> and the onions, and the garlick:

44

But now our soul is dried away: there is nothing at all, beside this manna, before our eyes.

And the manna was as coriander seed, and the colour thereof as the colour of bdellium.

And the people went about, and gathered it, and ground it in mills, or beat it in a mortar, and baked it in pans, and made cakes of it: and the taste of it was as the taste of fresh oil.

And when the dew fell upon the camp in the night, the manna fell upon it.

Then Moses heard the people weep throughout their families, every man in the door of his tent: and the anger of the Lord was kindled greatly; Moses also was displeased.

Numbers 11:4-10

Why were the people weeping? They were weeping because they didn't like their leadership. They thought they were being led astray. They didn't have the kind of food they wanted. All they had was heavenly bread! (Praise God.) They lusted after fish, cucumbers, melons, leeks, onions, and garlic.

They were weeping, feeling sorry for themselves. That lead to murmuring and complaining: "Moses, we want more and better food. Why did you bring us out here to this miserable place? We don't like it here. We don't like this manna; we're tired of it. We want to go back to Egypt; at least there we had some good things to eat. You have led us out here in this desert to die of starvation! Some leader you are!"

So what happened when they complained this way?

And there went forth a wind from the Lord, and brought quails from the sea, and let them fall by the camp, as it were a day's journey on this side, and as

45

it were a day's journey on the other side, round about
the camp, as it were two cubits upon the face of the
earth.

And the people stood up all that day, and all that
night, and all the next day, and they gathered the
quails: he that gathered least gathered ten homars: and
they spread them all abroad for themselves round
about the camp.

And while the flesh was yet between their teeth,
ere it was chewed, the wrath of the Lord was kindled
against the people, and the Lord smote the people with
a great plague.

Numbers 11:31-33

God let those people get that meat in their mouths,
get a good taste of it, and then He judged them for
speaking out against His leadership. God took it
personally when the people came against His chosen
leader. That should be a lesson to you and me. If we
can't agree with our leader, with the man or woman
of God — the apostle, evangelist, prophet, pastor or
teacher — then we should at least keep our mouths
shut. We should leave the church and go someplace
else— anything other than getting into an area that
would displease God and open the door for the devil
to steal, kill and destroy. Or even bring divine judgment upon us. Let me give you another example.

And, behold, there came a man of God out of
Judah by the word of the Lord unto Bethel: and
Jeroboam stood by the altar to burn incense.

And he cried against the altar in the word of the
Lord, and said, O altar, altar, thus saith the Lord;
Behold, a child shall be born unto the house of David,
Josiah by name; and upon thee shall he offer the
priests of the high places that burn incense upon thee,
and men's bones shall be burnt upon thee.

46

> And he gave a sign the same day, saying, This is the sign which the Lord hath spoken; Behold, the altar shall be rent, and the ashes that are upon it shall be poured out.
>
> And it came to pass, when king Jeroboam heard the saying of the man of God, which had cried against the altar in Bethel, that he *put forth his hand* from the altar, saying, *Lay hold on him.* And his hand, which he put forth against him, *dried up,* so that he could not pull it in again to him.
>
> **1 Kings 13:1-4**

It is dangerous coming against the ministry gifts. There have been so many like King Jeroboam. Because they didn't like the message taught or the form of administration in the church, or the decisions made, have tried to lay hold on the gift from God. King Jeroboam's hand dried up because of a wrong attitude.

I have been told of an individual who constantly criticized a particular ministry, publicly and otherwise, and had to be hospitalized with cancer of the tongue. I know of another situation where a man talked and fought against a ministry gift and was not open to correction. Soon afterwards, he was hospitalized, at the point of death, and it wasn't until he repented and the ministry gift he had so unwisely criticized prayed for him, that he was healed.

Don't be a part of Satan's plan to destroy you. Paul said, "We're not ignorant of Satan's devices." Remember Ananias and Sapphira? A part of their problem was not repecting the ministry gift.

God doesn't want us to murmur against the leaders in the Body of Christ. But there is more to this tune: God also doesn't want us to murmer against secular leaders. God just doesn't want us murmuring — period!

God doesn't want His people talking about the President of the United States, or the governor of the state, or the mayor of the city, or about any other duly authorized and instituted leader of our society — whether that leader is born again or not!

God wants us to have the proper attitude toward *all* those in positions of authority, whatever their race, religion, color, creed, or sex. What is the "proper" attitude toward those in authority? The Apostle Paul gives us some clue in 1 Timothy 2:1-4:

> I exhort therefore, that first of all, supplications, prayers, intercessions, and giving of thanks, be made for all men;
>
> For kings, and for all that are in authority; that we may lead a quiet and peaceable life in all godliness and honesty.
>
> For this is good and acceptable in the sight of God our Saviour.
>
> Who will have all men to be saved, and to come unto the knowledge of the truth.

Here we see that we are to *pray* for those who are in authority. God doesn't want us to criticize and oppose our spiritual, social, and political leaders; He wants us to pray for them, to intercede for them, to make good and positive confessions over them. However, when the opportunity arrives, through the political process, we need to exercise our rights to effect positive change.

Believers need to stop degrading and speaking derogatorily about their government and leaders and start lifting them up in prayer. We need to begin to say good things about them. Don't say what you don't want, say what you *do* want. Start saying things like, "Our leader is influenced by the Spirit of God."

48

Don't talk against or about any leader anywhere
. . . not negatively. Intercede and believe for his good
— and ours. Pray for him and all leaders everywhere
so we might live a quiet and peaceable life in all
godliness and honesty. This is good and acceptable in
the sight of God.

Are you ready to repent? Pray this prayer out loud:

"Heavenly Father, in the name of Jesus I ask You
to forgive me for coming against the ministry gifts and
secular leaders. Forgive me for my actions and words
that were contrary to Your Word. I receive my
forgiveness now in Jesus' name, and thank You for
cleansing me from all unrighteousness. I purpose in
my heart now to be a blessing, to receive the ministry
gifts as being from You, and to watch my words and
actions.

"Thank You for helping in these areas as I confess:
'I can do all things through Christ which strengtheneth
me.'

"In Jesus' name I believe I receive. Amen."

4

Know Your Leadership

And we beseech you, brethren, to know them which labour among you, and are over you in the Lord, and admonish you.

And to esteem them very highly in love for their work's sake. And be at peace among yourselves.

1 Thessalonians 5:12,13

The Amplified Bible version of this passage reads:

Now also we beseech you, brethren, get to know those who labor among you — recognize them for what they are, acknowledge and appreciate and respect them all — your leaders who are over you in the Lord, and those who warn and kindly reprove and exhort you.

And hold them in very high and most affectionate esteem in [intelligent and sympathetic] appreciation of their work. Be at peace among yourselves.

As members of the Body of Christ, the third attitude we should have is a determination to get to know our spiritual leader.

Now that doesn't mean that you have to go and eat in his house. It doesn't mean that you have to sit down with him every week and discuss the affairs of the church. It simply means that you need to take the time to get to know him as a man of God. It means that you need to make sure that what he is feeding you is the uncompromised Word of God.

You also need to, as much as is practical, take the time to be around your leader to observe his life, his conversation and the way he ministers to his own family. You need to know whether or not he is of God. When you go to hear him speak, you should take your Bible, a notebook and pencil or pen, and write down what he says. Note the scriptures he quotes or refers to. Look them up. Check to see if they really say and mean what he says they do.

In 2 Timothy 2:15, the Apostle Paul writes to young Timothy, **Study to shew thyself approved unto God, a workman that needeth not to be ashamed, rightly dividing the word of truth.** While the Greek word translated **study** here does not mean academic or scholastic effort or mental activity as it does to us today, the thrust of the verse is good advice. *The New International Version* translates this verse well when it says: ***Do your best to present yourself to God as one approved, a workman who does not need to be ashamed and who correctly handles the word of truth.***

One way to *correctly handle the word of truth* is to make sure that those who teach and explain it are themselves correctly handling it. We need to be very careful of who we allow to interpret scripture to us. We need to make sure that the scriptures they use as a basis for their doctrines and teaching are really in the Bible, are correctly quoted, and actually do mean what the teacher says they mean. Having verses lifted totally out of context and making them say something the writer never intended has done harm to the Body of Christ.

You and I need to make sure that what we are hearing is the truth, and not just the ideas, doctrines, and private interpretations of men. In order to do that, we must pay careful attention to what is being taught and the scriptural basis that is given for it. We need to ascertain for ourselves whether what our spiritual leader is proclaiming is the true and unadulterated Word of God. We do that not only by looking up the verses being presented but also by comparing them with the context from which they are taken and the whole context of the entire Bible.

A lot of Christians are going around quoting things that the Bible supposedly says, when those things are nowhere to be found in the Bible. Such people think that they are quoting the Bible because they are repeating what they have heard some man say from a pulpit someplace. They may go along for decades thinking they are quoting scripture, only to find out years later that what they have been quoting is nothing but some man's thoughts.

This kind of unquestioning trust in man demonstrates a wrong attitude. As Christians, we are nowhere told to let someone else do our reading, thinking, and studying for us. Each of us is personally responsible for determining the truth for himself or herself. You and I as believers ought to have the attitude, "I'm going to get to know my spiritual leader so I can know whether I can trust him to preach the unadulterated truth of God's Word."

If we are going to take part in any church organization or group, we need to know what is being preached there. We should watch, observe, note, and study for ourselves what is being set forth as God's truth. In Acts 17:11, we read that the people in Berea . . . **were more noble than those in Thessalonica, in that they received the word with all readiness of mind, and searched the scriptures daily,** (to determine) **whether those things** (preached) **were so.** Everybody is capable of making an error. Even you and I as believers. Even those who are called to the five-fold ministry. Therefore, it is our individual responsibility to make sure that what is being taught and preached is truly the pure milk of the Word of God.

One way to judge whether the message being set forth by a man or woman of God is true is to examine the fruit of that person's individual life. For example, if you were a part of the church which I pastor, you would not only need to check the accuracy of the message I preach, you would also want to observe my public, professional and personal behavior. You would want to observe the way I minister to my own family to see if it is in line with the Word of God. Because the Bible teaches that a person who can't rule his own household is not qualified to rule over the household of God (or any part of it). (1 Tim. 3:5.)

Now I'm not talking about perfection. Nobody is perfect. But if you were to see that my home life was totally out of control, that there was no love or harmony in it, that my children were running wild, that I was not raising them up properly, then you would have to conclude, "Well, that man preaches the Word of God all right, but he is still out of line." In that case, you would not be criticizing, judging, or condemning me. You would simply be doing what the Bible says for believers to do. We are to get to know our leaders, those who exercise spirtitual authority over us.

As a member of the Body of Christ, you ought to have an attitude that says, "I am going to take the time and put out the effort necessary to get to know my leader." If everything is in order, then you can feel free to "hook in" with that person and help him or her accomplish God's work in that place. You can dig in there and be a blessing. You can be assured that you are being part of the answer and not part of the problem.

A long time ago, I made the decision that I would never get behind a pulpit and preach the Word of God if my home was not in order. Today I can very honestly and openly declare that I have never regretted that decision or gone back on it. Any time I have stepped into the pulpit, I have done so with my home in order. When I arise to proclaim the Word of God, there is harmony in my home.

But besides getting to know our leaders to make sure that what they preach is the pure Word of God, besides checking to make sure that their personal lives are in order, we are also told by the Bible, . . . **be at peace among yourselves** (1 Thess. 5:13). You can be at peace with yourself only if you know that the one who exercises authority and rule over you is God's anointed, chosen by Him, in obedience to Him and in harmony with Him. If you are not sure whether or not a person is of God, you will have a hard time following him wholeheartedly. No one can follow another with all his heart unless he has the assurance that the one he is following is in the right — following Jesus.

By the same token, no one can lead others unless he is sure that those who follow him have complete confidence and trust in him and his leadership. But that confidence and trust have got to be founded on truth. The leader has got to prove himself worthy of trust and confidence.

Let's take Jim Jones for an example. Many people say he was wrong to lead all those people into destruction. Yes, he was wrong, there's no doubt about it. What

Jim Jones did was atrocious, it was terrible, and God hated it! I hate and detest it. I'm sure you do too. But so many times we have a tendency to condemn the leader and to lay total blame on him alone. But no leader can lead without followers. Those who follow a person have an obligation to check him out and to make sure that he is leading them in the right way. If that leader is not of God, then those who follow him have a responsibility to find that out and to refuse to be led off into error. We cannot lay all the blame for that destruction on Jim Jones; his followers were also to blame for not getting to know the person to whom they were entrusting their very lives.

You and I have a responsibility to know the person to whom we give allegiance and obedience. If the person you are now following is not of God, then you need to get out of that group or organization. If he or she is not preaching the truth, you must get out and find someone who is. If you know that what you are a part of is wrong, then it is your responsibility to do something about it. God will not only call that person to answer for what he taught you that was in error, He will also call you to answer for what you did about it.

"Why did you sit there and open your ears and mind and heart to that false teaching week after week?" the Lord may ask you.

"But, Father, I stayed there so I could sing in the choir . . . But, Father, I was a deacon (or Sunday School teacher, or usher, or songleader) . . . But, Father, it was the closest church to my home . . ."

The Lord is not going to accept those excuses. He sees that when we really want to, we always manage to find a way to get across town to do our shopping or play golf or attend a football game. He knows that if we really wanted to, we could find a church in which His Word is really being preached and practiced. We must accept responsibility for our attitudes and actions. One of those attitudes and actions includes the responsibility of getting to know our leader and of finding one who will lead us aright.

As a pastor, I want my people to know me. But I'm not going to invite them over to my house for dinner every day. That's not what I mean by getting to know me. I want them to examine my life both within the church and outside it. I want them to listen to me preach and to verify that what I teach is so. I also want them to see that I practice what I preach and teach.

The Bible tells us that where there is no vision, the people perish. (Prov. 29:18.) I want my people to find out if I have a vision or not. If I don't, then I want them to get out of the church, because I will just be leading them in a circle. The blind only lead the blind into a ditch.

You need to know whether your leader has a vision or not. You must not just go to some church and blindly accept anything and everything that is preached there. Find out whether the message being presented is true. Examine it in light of the scriptures. Test it by the Holy Spirit Who indwells you. Find out whether the person in charge has a vision for his church. If your spiritual leader has no real zeal and enthusiasm, no real plans for growth and expansion and reaching out to touch lives for Christ, then I would say that you should leave that church. Because where there is no vision, the people perish.

Let's look at 1 Thessalonians 5:13 in *The Amplified Bible* again: **And hold them in very high and most affectionate esteem in [*intelligent* and sympathetic] appreciation of their work . . . .** God wants us to be *intelligent* about leadership. That means that although we are not to judge and condemn our leaders (or anyone else), we *are* to examine their words and lifestyle. Because it is by its fruit that a tree is known. Don't judge anyone's heart, but do take the Word and Spirit of God and examine what he is saying and doing. Examine his speech and his lifestyle. It is righteous judgment (spiritual discernment) to examine leadership in light of the Word of God.

In Romans 13:7 the Apostle Paul writes: **Render therefore to all their dues; tribute to whom tribute is due; custom to whom custom; fear to whom fear; honour to whom honour.**

When you have gotten to know your leader, recognized that what he is teaching is the Word of God, and verified (to the best of your ability) that his personal lifestyle is in line with that Word — then you can render unto him what is rightfully due him. And what is rightfully due him? *Respect.* And *submission.* That is the next attitude.

Keep in mind that I am talking about the office of apostle, prophet, evangelist, pastor and teacher. You shouldn't support a ministry just because it is called a ministry. You should know whether or not the person in charge of it is of God or not. If your leaders are of God, then you should hold them in very high and affectionate esteem for who and what they are. And who are they? God's anointed. What are they? They're His gifts to the Church.

The Bible teaches us to get to know our spiritual leaders. Then after we get to know them, we should have the attitude of submission or obedience.

5
Submission

Remember them which have the rule over you, who have spoken unto you the word of God: whose faith follow, considering the end of their conversation.

Hebrews 13:7

The Greek word translated **rule** in this verse refers to shepherd-like authority. So we are admonished by the writer to remember those who have shepherd-like authority over us. Now notice verse 17 of that same chapter:

> **Obey them that have the rule over you, and submit yourselves: for they watch for your souls, as they that must give account, that they may do it with joy, and not with grief: for that is unprofitable for you.**

This verse stresses the next attitude which we are to have toward those who are in spiritual authority over us; we are to have an attitude of *submission* or obedience. We can do that only when we know our leaders — not before.

Once you are convinced that your leaders are men and women of God, then you can submit yourself to them. When you are sure that they teach nothing but the Word of God, when they have demonstrated to you that their personal lives are in order, when they have shown that they have control over their mouths, when you have determined for yourself that they have a vision — then you can "hook in" with them and be the blessing you know the Lord intends for you to be in that place of service.

We have seen that those who "rule" over us exercise "shepherd-like authority." In order for there to be a shepherd, there must be sheep. What is the function of sheep in regard to their shepherd? They are to *follow* him.

David was a shepherd lad. Before becoming king over Israel, David led sheep. Sheep follow. But goats kick . . . and bite . . . and butt. Many of those who claim to be the Lord's sheep are really goats, because they are forever butting — "But . . . but . . . but . . .!" God has not called His shepherds to lead goats! If you are out of fellowship with the leadership in your particular church, then you are in the wrong fold. Goats fellowship with goats, and sheep fellowship with sheep. You need to find the fold in which you can fellowship with other sheep.

Besides fellowship, there is also "follow-ship." Sheep need a shepherd to lead them. The Chief Shepherd has provided His sheep with under-shepherds for that purpose. The Lord's sheep need to be able to give the same allegiance and obedient "follow-ship" to His appointed under-shepherds that they give to Him.

If you find that you cannot give "follow-ship" to your shepherd because he himself is not following the Chief Shepherd, then you need to change flocks. Notice that I did *not* say that you need to rebel against that leadership. It is never necessary to rebel against the ministry gifts.

In Acts 5 we read where the disciples were brought before the Jewish council because they were preaching the Gospel against orders. The council was considering punishing them severely. Let's see what happened:

> Then stood there up one in the council, a Pharisee, named Gamaliel, a doctor of the law, had in reputation among all the people, and commanded to put the apostles forth a little space;
>
> And said unto them, Ye men of Israel, take heed to yourselves what ye intend to do . . . .
>
> . . . Refrain from these men, and let them alone: for if this counsel or this work be of men, it will come to nought:
>
> But if it be of God, ye cannot overthrow it; lest haply ye be found even to fight against God.
>
> Acts 5:34,35,38,39

You and I can learn a valuable lesson here. We never have to come against a leader who says he is of God. We can just leave him alone. If his ministry is of man, it will come to nothing. (Jim Jones was of man; he and his ministry both came to nothing.) However, if the ministry is of God, both he and it will stand and will win out over every storm, every obstacle, every form of opposition and persecution. It will win! If we oppose it, we can end up fighting against God!

The writer of Hebrews warns us to obey those who have the rule over us. Remember that the word *rule* here refers to "shepherd-like authority." A shepherd loves his sheep. Jesus, the Chief Shepherd, is a lover. God is love. Those whom He chooses and anoints must be like Him; they too must love. Don't follow anyone who doesn't love you. If you're not convinced that the man in charge loves you, don't follow him, because there is usually a reason you are not convinced of his love for you.

Now I would hope that the reason you are convinced he doesn't love you is *not* because he doesn't stand at the door of the church and shake your hand as you leave. I would also hope it isn't because he won't allow you to "button-hole" him after every service and occupy his valuable time with your long-winded tales or complaints. Those things are not indications of a lack of love on your pastor's part, they point to your own pettiness and immaturity. Even if your pastor doesn't placate you and pander to you, if he is available to you in time of real need, then that demonstrates his love for you.

A shepherd loves his sheep; he ministers to them in love. Every now and then he has to get firm with them, because sometimes they want to go wandering away and he has to pull them back. You will find that a real shepherd sometimes has to use his rod on the sheep in order to teach the errant ones to stay away from danger. The "rod" which the pastor-shepherd uses on his flock is the Word of God. Sometimes he has to administer that Word in ways that may seem harsh and cruel, but it is not his purpose or intention to harm the flock. On the contrary, he is simply exercising authority and rule over them to keep them from harming themselves and each other. If you can't stand to be corrected by the Word of God spoken in love by your pastor-shepherd, then you need to find yourself another sheepfold.

Notice that I said "corrected by the Word of God spoken *in love.*" It is not my advice to follow a pastor who uses his pulpit as a whipping block. That's not shepherd-like authority. Trying to "get back" at the flock from the pulpit is not exercising God-given authority in love. I wouldn't follow that type leadership if I were in your place. The pulpit should be used to teach the Word of God.

Wouldn't it be terrible if you weren't sure whether or not your leader was a hopeless gossip or an alcoholic or a drug addict or a whoremonger or a wife beater or a child molester? You wouldn't be at peace with yourself in that situation, would you? However, when you know that he is none of these things, but a good, moral man who can be trusted, then you will have confidence in him and his leadership.

Even if you do have a legitimate disagreement with your leader, you can still submit to him if you know that he is of God. You may not see eye to eye on everything — you probably won't — but you can at least disagree *agreeably.* You can pray and intercede for him because you are convinced that he is a man of God, open to the Spirit of God. If this is the case and he is in the wrong, you can be assured that his Boss will straighten him out! But you cannot take it upon yourself to set him straight! He is not *your* servant, he is the Lord's. You would do well to leave God's servant alone and let the Lord do the correcting that is needed. Otherwise, you will find yourself "fighting against God," and then *you* will end up being the one being set straight!

For too long now the Church has gone the way of the world. When things go wrong in the local church body, we'll gripe and complain, fuss and fight, vie for control of the church, call upon the deacons or elders to set the pastor straight, appeal to the bishop or other church authorities to vindicate us against our "adversary," circulate rumors and gossip and petitions against our leaders. I've even heard of instances in which church members have filed law suits against each other or their leader, called in the police to get their way, or even brought guns to church with them! Some have rebelled and taken a group out to start a new church in retaliation. Can you believe that Christians can get so far from the central message of the Gospel — which is love?

We must realize that nothing positive ever comes out of these kinds of decisions. Learning to be in obedience to the Lord and to His anointed and ordained leaders will bring the harmony Jesus prayed that His Church would have. (John 17:21).

Obey them that have the rule over you, and submit yourselves: *for they watch for your souls . . . .* (Heb. 13:17). Understand that pastors have an awesome responsibility. Some people want to be in the ministry because they mistakenly think it has great glory attached to it. Personally, there have been times when I have asked the Lord, "O God, why me; why did You call *me* to this task?" Being part of the ministry gift to the Church is awesome. It is an awesome responsibility to be called to deal with so many different personalities and such a variety of attitudes and outlooks.

Finally you reach a point in the ministry where you just have to accept that not everyone is going to agree — with you or with each other. You realize that you are going to have to love them all, and go on about your business.

As a pastor, I have to watch for the souls of those in my charge. One day I will have to stand before the Father and give account for each of the sheep placed in my care. I have a great responsibility. That's why everything that comes forth from me — especially when I am in that pulpit — has to be from God. I can't just step in front of a congregation and scatter shoot, hoping that some of it will hit the mark. I have to make every shot count. I must make certain that I am hitting the bull's-eye every time.

Neither can I just give the people what they like. When it comes to spiritual food, I must feed the flock a balanced diet, one that is best for them. Regardless of their personal tastes and preferences, I have to feed them a full-course meal. God doesn't want His sheep to be just skin and bones, He wants them to have some meat on those bones. But you don't build spiritual muscles from spiritual popcorn! Therefore, as a pastor it is my duty to stand before my congregation and offer them the full-balanced diet of the real meat of the Word — whether they like or want it or not.

I am responsbile for what I say and do with the Lord's flock. I must give an account for the words that come from my mouth, for the counsel I have given in my office and over the phone, and for the life I have lived before the people. Every ministry gift will have to give account. That responsibility and accountability is not something we in the ministry take lightly. It is an awesome assignment.

When I was called into the ministry, my grandfather said to me, "Son, I have just one thing to tell you. From now on, people who have never paid you any attention will start watching every move you make. All eyes are going to be upon you, because you have said that you are called of God."

People don't watch the sheep nearly as closely as they watch the shepherd. If a person stands in the office of apostle, prophet, evangelist, pastor or teacher, he will be watched like a hawk.

Obey them that have the rule over you, and submit yourselves: for they watch for your souls, *as they that must give account* **. . . .** The ministry gifts must give account for themselves. But they are not the only ones: **. . . that they may do it with joy, and not with grief: for that is unprofitable for you.** Those who make up the flock will also have to give account for how they treated God's gifts to His Church.

In this verse, the Lord is telling us to be sure that we are in the place we are supposed to be in so we can allow the man or woman of God to lead us with joy. If we make it hard on our spiritual leaders, it will be unprofitable for us — not for *them,* but for us.

The Lord warns us to follow spiritual leadership, to submit and be obedient to it so our leaders can lead us with joy and not with grief. Moses shepherded with grief. The children of Israel griped and complained against him and the Lord constantly. They murmured and murmured until finally Moses cried out to God to kill him because he was fed up with trying to lead such a crowd of hard-headed, stiff-necked, rebellious people. Let's look at his exact words in Numbers 11:11-15:

> **And Moses said unto the Lord, Wherefore hast thou afflicted thy servant? and wherefore have I not found favour in thy sight, that thou layest the burden of all this people upon me?**
>
> **Have I conceived all this people? have I begotten them, that thou shouldest say unto me, Carry them in thy bosom, as a nursing father beareth the sucking child, unto the land which thou swearest unto their fathers?**
>
> **Whence should I have flesh to give unto all this people? for they weep unto me, saying, Give us flesh, that we may eat.**

I am not able to bear all this people alone, because it is too heavy for me.

And if thou deal thus with me, kill me, I pray thee, out of hand, if I have found favour in thy sight; and let me not see my wretchedness.

So Moses reached a point where he said, "I'm just not able to take this any more." He came to that point because he was exercising leadership in grief. He said to the Lord, "If I have to continue leading these people like this, it will kill me. If it has to be this way, then I beg of You to go ahead and take my life now; get it over with so I can have some peace."

So the Lord, in essence, called for seventy elders of the people and anointed them to help Moses to lead the people with joy.

The point is, if you and I make it hard for our leaders, the Lord reminds us that our actions will be unprofitable for us. In other words, we will not succeed as we should in life. To *profit* means "to gain." To be unprofitable is to lose. If we disrespect our spiritual leadership, in some way or another we will lose. For the nation of Israel, their hardness of heart and rebellious attitude caused many of them to suffer sickness, disease and premature death.

When I speak of an attitude of submission or obedience to authority, I am not referring to extreme submission to another person. Some years ago there arose a doctrine in certain circles of the Church that believers were to turn over complete control of their lives to their pastors. These people could make no decisions on their own, not even about personal and family matters such as buying a car, purchasing a new home, changing churches — even taking a vacation! No!

That is not what is meant by submission to spiritual authority. No man has a right to make such personal decisions as that for you or me or anyone else. That is false doctrine and is based on selfishness, not spirituality.

For example, some religious leaders don't want their followers to go to any meetings outside of their own particular denomination or sect or group. That is not a valid exercise of spiritual authority. Those in the ministry gifts may be led of the Lord to warn their congregations about certain doctrines or practices which they believe to be false or dangerous, but they have no right to attempt to force anyone either to accept their views or to keep them from being exposed to other points of view. Submitting to spiritual leadership or authority does not imply a person's giving up his God-given right and responsibility to think for himself.

One particular man of God had the gall to try to tell all the married couples in his church when they could have sexual relations with each other. That is not of God. Neither is it of God when a person stands up in a meeting and, without any scriptural foundation for his remarks, tries to tell the ladies how long their dresses should be or whether they can wear make-up or not.

So when I speak of submission or obedience to spiritual authority, I am not speaking of such extremes as these mentioned here. Such practices are not evidences of spiritual leadership, they are man-made bondages.

However, the writer of Hebrews does instruct believers to *obey* those who have the rule over us and to submit ourselves to them, because they watch over our souls and must give account for us; therefore, we ought to submit to their authority that they might lead with joy.

Now notice the Apostle Paul's remarks in 1 Corinthians 16:15:

> **I beseech you, brethren, (ye know the house of Stephanas, that it is the firstfruits of Achaia, and that they have** *addicted themselves* **to the ministry of the saints).**

Now that is a good addiction. Do you want to get "hooked" on something good? Then do as the family of Stephanas and get "hooked" on ministering to the Body of Christ. Get "hooked" on being a blessing to your brothers and sisters in the Lord. Get addicted to that kind of loving service and you'll never get bored or depressed or find yourself without the necessities of life. Instead, you'll find happiness, joy, fulfillment and overflowing abundance. Why? Because you'll be operating in the law of Luke 6:38: **Give, and it shall be given unto you; good measure, pressed down, and shaken together, and running over, shall men give into your bosom. For with the same measure that ye mete withal it shall be measured to you again.**

Notice Paul's words 1 Corinthians 16:16:

> (I beseech you, brethren) **that ye submit yourselves unto such** (people as Stephanas and his family), **and to every one that helpeth with us, and laboureth.**

Here again Paul is talking about submission. But notice that he first recognizes the character of the individuals to whom his readers should submit themselves. He emphasizes that they are those who have "addicted" themselves to the ministry of the saints, and are laboring with Paul and his co-workers in the ministry. Paul knows the ones who are laboring with him. He is not telling his readers to submit to just anyone. He knows these people, this household, personally. That's why he knows he is safe in urging his readers to submit themselves to them. He knows they can be trusted to correctly exercise spiritual authority.

The Bible teaches very clearly in Mark 3 that Satan does not fight against himself. Jesus said: "A house divided against itself cannot stand." So it is important that you and I know that those who have rule over us are credible so we can submit ourselves and not divide the "house." If a local church or fellowship is divided against itself, it will fall. God wants His people to be like-minded, to work, worship and fellowship together as one.

There is tremendous power in unity. It is important that Christians have an attitude of oneness in the Lord. I personally don't want to be part of a divided fellowship, one, for example, that doesn't believe in healing, while its pastor does — or vice versa. In such a situation, how could there possibly be agreement in prayer for healing? Suppose the pastor does not pray for healing because he is not sure that it is God's will to heal everyone. Someone in the church may begin to say, "The pastor doesn't know as much as I do, because I know God is a healer. He healed my body. The Bible says that God heals. That pastor is ignorant, therefore he can't be God's anointed!" Such words are divisive. The person who speaks them is dividing the house of the Lord. He is coming against God's anointed. The Bible says such action is unprofitable.

When we speak of submission or obedience to spiritual authority, we simply mean "hooking" in with the man (or woman) of God and with his God-given calling, anointing, and vision. We may not agree with him 100% of the time, but if we know that the Lord has placed us there in that fellowship, and that He has placed that leader there also, then we must submit to that God-chosen leader or else find ourselves to be fighting against God. We can disagree, but it must be *agreeably.* We must still walk in love. We must not complain, argue, or cause disturbances in that congregation. If we want to prosper and succeed in life, we must remain teachable. We must always be open to the leadership of the Holy Spirit so He can instruct us and show us where we are wrong.

Be ye followers of me, even as I also am of Christ.

1 Corinthians 11:1

Here Paul urges his readers to follow him, but only as long as he follows the Lord. That holds true for me as a pastor. I only want my people to follow me as long as what I'm preaching and practicing is the Word of God. As long as I am living a life that is holy, pure, upright, and consistent with the standards, principles, and concepts of the Word of God, then my people should give me the respect that is due the anointed of the Lord. However, if I get off into error, they should not feel obligated to follow me into it. You do not follow a person when he gets off the track!

I tell my congregation that if ever I get away from the Word of God, then it's time for them to leave. I warn them to follow me only as long as I follow Christ. If at any time my lifestyle gets out of line with the Word of the Lord, it's time for them to find some other spiritual leader to follow.

73

I also teach them that as long as they are a part of this fellowship which I have been called of the Lord to lead, and as long as I preach and practice the Word of the Lord, then they should give due respect, allegiance, and obedience to my leadership. I urge them to submit themselves to my leadership, to catch the vision the Lord has given me as His servant responsible for their welfare and instruction, and to cooperate with me in bringing that vision to pass.

Now that doesn't mean that they should give up and quit the church just because I make a mistake. We should abandon spiritual leadership *only* when that leadership shows a *consistent tendency* to go astray, to go contrary to the Word of God. In that case, it is dangerous to remain, because if we do we will be led into the same error. These matters call for serious consideration, mature judgment and a prayerful decision.

In Luke 16:12 Jesus tells us, . . . **if ye have not been faithful in that which is another man's, who shall give you that which is your own?** If you have not been faithful in that which belongs to another man, then who will give you what rightfully belongs to you?

So many people are looking for their own ministry. They are looking to be placed in a leadership position, to be given authority. The fact is, until a person learns how to follow, he will never lead!

Some people wonder why they are passed over at promotion time, even though they have been on the job longer than those who are promoted. The reason usually is that they have not been found faithful in what belongs to another man (the company). Until you and I learn to be faithful in another person's ministry, the

Lord is not going to give us our own ministry. The Body of Christ must learn to submit to authority.

Until you can "hook in" and follow someone else's leading, you're never going to be a leader yourself — no matter how much you may want to be. There are some people who are called of God to minister the Word of the Lord, but they haven't submitted to their pastor. They haven't been faithful in the little things, so they'll never be entrusted with the big things. If I were you, I wouldn't let that happen to me. I would learn to submit and be faithful in little so I can be trusted with much.

Some people are asked by their pastors to take responsibility for carrying out some project. Then later on the pastor discovers that they have been doing exactly opposite of everything he has taught them. He finds that they have been operating totally contrary to his instructions. They figured they knew better than the man of God, or had something burning in their spirit, so they went behind his back and did just opposite of what he had asked them to do. People who do that are not serving the Lord, but rather, promoting themselves. The Bible warns against this kind of attitude, saying that only those who can follow will ever be trusted to lead.

In 1 Corinthians 4:17, the Apostle Paul wrote to the church in Corinth:

> **For this cause have I sent unto you Timotheus, who is my beloved son, and faithful in the Lord, who shall bring you into remembrance *of my ways* which be in Christ, as I teach every where in every church.**

Notice what Paul was able to say about Timothy. He called him his (spiritual) "son," and stressed that he was *faithful*. Then he went on to say that Timothy would bring them into remembrance of *his* (Paul's) *ways*. So Paul is sending Timothy to these people in Corinth to remind them of Paul's ways! In other words, Timothy was going to say and do exactly what Paul would have said and done had he been there physically among them. Timothy was not sent to Corinth to talk behind Paul's back, to find fault with him, to spread rumors or gossip about him. He was not sent to build himself up at Paul's expense. He was sent to represent the man of God and to bring the people his words and message.

If I send people (with instructions) to speak for me and they take it upon themselves to preach something totally different from my message, that is not faithfulness on the part of those messengers. They cannot say to themselves, "Oh, I feel that Pastor Gool has missed it, so I think I'll do it my way. I have a better idea. I'll preach what I want to preach instead of what he sent me out to proclaim."

Did you know that God honors authority? He honors leadership. If I were to ask my assistant pastor to preach next Sunday on Proper Attitudes Toward Leadership, do you know what God would expect him to do? To preach on what I asked him to speak on. God is a God of authority and leadership, a God of faithfulness. Like the Apostle Paul who had every expectation that Timothy would do exactly what he was sent to Corinth to do, so also God expects His servants to do exactly what is requested and required of them.

In writing to the church in Philippi, Paul says this about Timothy:

> **But I trust in the Lord Jesus to send Timotheus unto you, that I also may be of good comfort, when I know your state.**
>
> **For I have no man likeminded, who will naturally care for your state.**
>
> **For all seek their own, not the things which are Jesus Christ's.**
>
> **Philippians 2:19-21**

That quality of faithfulness or submission is what made Timothy one of the greatest preachers in the early Church. He became one of the outstanding ministers and church leaders of his day because he first knew how to follow. He knew how to "hook in" with another man's anointing and to help him bring his God-given vision to fulfillment. Timothy proved himself faithful to the ministry of Paul, and when the time was right God rewarded Timothy by giving him his own great ministry.

6
Support — Financial

Once these four basic attitudes toward leadership are established, then there are three different areas of *support* which need to be provided to those in positions of spiritual leadership: 1) financial support, 2) prayer support, and 3) physical support.

Let's examine financial support first.

> Let the elders that rule well be counted worthy of double honour, especially they who labour in the word and doctrine.
>
> For the scripture saith, Thou shalt not muzzle the ox that treadeth out the corn. And, The labourer is worthy of his reward.
>
> 1 Timothy 5:17,18

The Amplified Bible version of this passage reads this way:

> Let the elders who perform the duties of their office well be considered doubly worthy of honor [and of adequate financial support], especially those who labor faithfully in preaching and teaching.
>
> For the Scripture says, You shall not muzzle an ox when it is treading out the grain, and again, The laborer is worthy of his hire.

One evidence of a proper attitude toward spiritual leadership is a willingness to provide adequate financial support for that leadership. If we know that a man or woman is of God and has been set up as our spiritual leader, then we owe that person the right to expect to be adequately paid.

In Galatians 6:6, the Apostle Paul writes:

Let him that is taught in the word communicate unto him that teacheth in all good things.

Again, *The Amplified Bible* translates this verse:

Let him who receives instruction in the Word [of God] share all good things with his teacher — contributing to his support.

In other words, we are not to eat at McDonald's and then get up and go pay at Wendy's! We are to pay where we are fed. We are to *contribute* to the financial welfare and support of the one who feeds us spiritually, the one who faithfully teaches us the Word and ways of the Lord.

You see, I don't believe the Bible teaches us that the man or woman of God who devotes full-time to the ministry should have to work eight-hours a day on a secular job to support himself or herself. Many people in the Body of Christ expect their spiritual leader to work a regular 40-hour-per-week job just as they do, and then to serve as spiritual leader in addition to their paid work. That is neither scriptural nor reasonable. No one can operate effectively in the ministry if he has to devote the bulk of his time to earning his own living and then serve the ministry on "overtime." That is asking too much. I assure you that Christian ministry is a full-time occupation, and should be rewarded as such financially. That means the minister is to be paid in full for ministry, so that outside work is not necessary.

So many church members wonder why their pastor doesn't have more to share with them on Sunday morning than he does. Often the reason is simple: he has been so busy working to earn a living and ministering to the needs of others, he has simply not had the time needed to devote to prayer, Bible reading, meditation and communion with the Lord. The Bible teaches that a workman, a laborer, is worthy of his hire (his wages). It also teaches that the one who benefits from spiritual teaching should contribute to the one who provides him that instruction.

I am a pastor and I don't punch a time clock. I don't work eight hours a day on a secular job. I devote full-time to my church. Therefore, my congregation has every right to expect me to provide them with quality teaching and preaching every service. As a church member, you have a right to expect your pastor to provide you that kind of service — *if* he or she is free to devote full-time to the church.

It is true that many pastors work outside their churches. I would hope that the reason they are doing so is because the Lord has instructed them to work a regular job, and not because they have to work to support themselves and their family or because they are driven by a love of money.

If your pastor is employed full-time in the ministry, then you have a right to expect him or her to devote full-time to that ministry. If he is not paid enough by the ministry to support him adequately and therefore has to take on a regular job, then you have no right to expect quality ministry from him. He simply won't have the time or energy to provide it.

The "bottom line" is: *If you adequately support your pastor financially, then he can adequately feed you spiritually.*

If your pastor desires to walk in the calling and anointing of God and to fulfill that which God has placed in his heart, then he should be allowed to do so. But he can't do that if his people are stingy!

In my opinion, one of the worst things that ever happened in the Church of Jesus Christ was the decision to put pastors on a set salary. The Bible doesn't teach this practice. The Bible teaches that the one who receives spiritual instruction should share with the one who provides that instruction. The implication is that the one who is blessed should be willing to share those blessings *proportionately* with the one who made them possible.

Now in reality, in many churches today the pastor is paid as little as the people can get away with. So many church leaders of our day live like the man described by Fred Price — on "Barely Get Along Street right next door to Grumble Alley." The reason they are grumbling is because they are barely getting along! And the reason they are barely getting along is because their people simply will not support them as they should. That is a shame.

It is a shame upon the Church of Jesus Christ when His chosen, ordained, anointed ministers are forced to lead lives of mediocrity or near the poverty level simply because His people are too stingy to share His blessings with the very ones who help make those blessing possible. Ministers of the Lord give their lives to their people. These devoted servants of the Lord ought to live well.

When a man of God is preaching and teaching the Word of God, loving and caring for the sheep in his care, giving counsel when needed, leading his people in the things of God, then he ought to be blessed by those people. These quality, competent leaders should be blessed by believers.

I believe that ideally pastors should not be put on a set salary, but rather paid in proportion to the blessings that are produced among the people. Granted, this could be a reality in a set salary situation, if the finance board has ended up requesting or begging for the pastor's salary to be raised. What a precarious position to be in. If the people are being blessed financially, they can be afforded the opportunity to share those blessing proportionately with the ministry gift. One way to do that is to allow each member to prayerfully designate a portion of his tithes to the pastor and his family. If the people are being fed well, then they in turn should feed their pastor well. That is scriptural. The biblical responsibility of the sheep is to "communicate" (share with) the one who ministers to them. Why take the chance of subjecting the ministry gift to a board that may not like him or is stingy or selfish?

Of course, the pastor has to know that his source is God and never the people. But the way God has chosen to pour out His blessings upon us is through other people. One way He has chosen to bless His ordained servants is through those who benefit from their ministry.

> **Am I not an apostle? am I not free? have I not seen Jesus Christ our Lord? are not ye my work in the Lord?**
>
> **If I be not an apostle unto others, yet doubtless I am to you: for the seal of mine apostleship are ye in the Lord.**
>
> **1 Corinthians 9:1,2**

Here Paul writes to the church he established in Corinth. He says to them: "Am I not an apostle, at least to *you?* Other people may not recognize me as an apostle of the Lord Jesus Christ, but surely you should. Because it was I who came and preached the Gospel to you, ministered to you, got you saved and healed and set free. You should *know* that I am a man of God."

That is a good point. No matter what anybody else may think or say about a ministry that you support, you should know for yourself that that ministry or minister is of God. If you are supporting a particular ministry or minister, you shouldn't let anyone else's opinion affect you in the least. If you hear someone say something against that person or work, just ignore what they say and go right on with your faithful support. Don't let the opinions of others shake your resolve or commitment. Know whom and what you believe, and be faithful.

Notice also that Paul says that the Corinthians are his "seal of apostleship." That is, they are the *evidence* that Paul is a true apostle.

> Mine answer to them that do examine me is this,
>
> Have we not power to eat and to drink?
>
> Have we not power to lead about a sister, a wife, as well as other apostles, and as the brethren of the Lord, and Cephas?
>
> Or I only and Barnabas, have not we power to forbear working?
>
> 1 Corinthians 9:3-6

What Paul is saying here is: "Since Barnabas and I are also apostles, then we ought to have the same right to keep a wife and to be financially supported as the others, like Peter." Evidently Peter took his wife along with him on some evangelistic trips and the people he ministered to provided for their needs. As an apostle, Paul was pointing out that he should and did have the same right to such provision. He didn't think that he and Barnabas should be singled out to work on their own to support themselves, when the other apostles were supported by the people.

Who goeth a warfare any time at his own charges?
who planteth a vineyard, and eateth not of the fruit
thereof? or who feedeth a flock, and eateth not of the
milk of the flock?

1 Corinthians 9:7

Again Paul illustrates his point by saying:
"Whoever heard of a soldier going to war and having
to pay his own expenses? Or whoever plants a garden
without the right to eat from it? If you have ever tilled
the ground, planted seed, cultivated and harvested
crops, then you know how much work that is. Didn't
you expect to benefit from what you were working
so hard to produce? No one raises animals with no
expectation of making a living from them. Why should
it be any different with us who labor in the Lord's
vineyard, or among His flock?"

Say I these things as a man? or saith not the law
the same also?

1 Corinthians 9:8

"Do you think I'm saying this on my own, that I
am making this up? Doesn't the law say the same
thing?":

For it is written in the law of Moses, Thou shalt
not muzzle the mouth of the ox that treadeth out the
corn. Doth God take care for oxen?

Or saith he it altogether for our sakes? For our
sakes, no doubt, this is written: that he that ploweth
should plow in hope, and that he that thresheth in
hope should be partaker of his hope.

1 Corinthians 9:9,10

In other words, Paul is asking, "Did God write this
just for oxen? Did He really mean for this command-
ment to be applied just to animals? Or was He refer-

ring to ministry gifts when He said that the one who works ought to be fed from that work?"

> If we have sown unto you spiritual things, is it a great thing if we shall reap your carnal things?
>
> If others be partakers of this power over you, are not we rather? Nevertheless we have not used this power; but suffer all things, lest we should hinder the gospel of Christ.
>
> 1 Corinthians 9:11,12

"If we have sown spiritual things in you, then don't we have every right to reap material things from you?" asks Paul. "If others take advantage of this power to reap from you, then don't we, of all people, have the same right? But we have not used this power."

Why? Why had Paul and Barnabas not taken advantage of their right to receive their physical living from the ones in Corinth to whom they had shared spiritual life? Because these men of God didn't want to do anything that might cause the Gospel to be spoken ill of at that time.

> Do ye not know that they which minister about holy things live of the things of the temple? and they which wait at the altar are partakers with the altar?
>
> Even so hath the Lord ordained that they which preach the gospel should live of the gospel.
>
> 1 Corinthians 9:13,14

Once you are in the place that God wants you to be in, then you ought to support financially the man or woman of God who is charged with the responsibility of leading that ministry. If that person ministers to you spiritual things, then you should turn around and minister physical, material things to him or her.

A man of God should not have to be concerned about how he is going to make a living. If he is ministering the Word of God, walking in his calling, then the people he leads ought to supply him with a living. The ones who benefit from spiritual leadership should be the ones who provide the necessities of that spiritual leadership. That is their spiritual obligation and responsibility. That is their part in the ministry of their leader.

In *The Amplified Bible* version of Philippians 4:14-17 we read these words from Paul addressed to the believers in Philippi:

> But it was right and commendable and noble of you to contribute for my needs and to share my difficulties with me.
>
> And you Philippians yourselves well know that in the early days of the Gospel ministry, when I left Macedonia, no church (assembly) *entered into partnership with me* and opened up [a debit and credit] account in giving and receiving except you only.
>
> For even in Thessalonica you sent [me contributions] for my needs, not only once but a second time.
>
> Not that I seek or am eager for [your] gift, but I do seek and am eager for the fruit which increases to your credit — the harvest of blessing that is accumulating to your account.

Notice what Paul is saying here. He is speaking to people who have supported his ministry, people who have received from him spiritual things and from whom he has received material support in the past. He says that by their action of giving and receiving, these people had become partners in his ministry.

When someone ministers to you the Word of God, the life of God, you ought to minister life in return. The Spirit of God says that by doing that you actually open up a debit and credit account, a giving and receiving with that ministry.

Then Paul goes on in verses 18,19:

> But I have [your full payment] and more; I have everything I need and am amply supplied, now that I have received from Epaphroditus the gifts you sent me. [They are the] fragrant odor [of] an offering and sacrifice which God welcomes and in which He delights.
>
> And my God will liberally supply (fill to the full) your every need according to His riches in glory in Christ Jesus.

Here Paul promises God's abundant supply. But notice to whom he was giving this promise. He wasn't speaking to just anybody and everybody. He was speaking specifically to those who were walking in the principles of God's Word, those who were giving into the ministry of the Gospel.

The principle involved here is, "To the one who ministers to you spiritual things is owed material things." These people were being blessed by receiving from Paul great spiritual blessings; therefore, they owed him a portion of their material blessings. The more they blessed him materially, the more they received in return.

Because Paul had so blessed them, they said to him: "Paul, since you've been so good to us, we want to help you. We're going to help you to fulfill your God-given vision. We're going to assist you so you can go from one place to another and spread the Good News so others can be blessed as we have been. You have blessed us, so we are going to bless you."

By doing so, Paul says that they had opened up a heavenly bank account. They had become partners with him in the ministry the Lord had given him. That's why he told them that his God would supply their every need from His riches in glory by Christ Jesus.

You see, not just anyone can quote Philippians 4:19 and expect it to come true in his life. Anyone can "confess" that "my God shall supply all MY needs." However, unless he is a regular partner in the ministry of the Gospel, he has no basis for making that statement. Unless a person has opened a heavenly bank account by investing in the ministry, he has no assets to draw upon — he is spiritually bankrupt.

This verse is for those who are in partnership with the ministry of the Gospel of Jesus Christ, as the Philippians were. This is a promise to those who are supporting their spiritual leader, as the church in Philippi was supporting Paul. If you are in partnership with the ministry to which God has led you, then you can say, "My God will supply all my needs according to His riches in glory by Christ Jesus." On the other hand, if you are not a giver, if your pastor or spiritual leader is starving because you are too stingy to support him, then you have no right to expect to receive anything from the One who supports you. You can "confess" day in and day out that God supplies all your needs, but if you are not depositing into your heavenly bank account, then you have no reserves to draw upon.

Jesus had this principle operative in His ministry also. Notice Luke 8:1-3:

> And it came to pass afterward, that he went throughout every city and village, preaching and shewing the glad tidings of the kingdom of God: and the twelve were with him.
>
> And certain women, which had been healed of evil spirits and infirmities, Mary called Magdalene, out of whom went seven devils,

And Joanna the wife of Chuza Herod's steward, and Susanna, and many others, which *ministered unto him of their substance.*

We must put first things first. And guess what? *Self* is not first! The kingdom of God is first. The things of God are first. Obeying God's Word is first. Unless we put the kingdom of God and His righteousness *first* in our lives, we have no right to expect to receive "all these other things" we expect "to be added unto" us.

Furthermore David the king said unto all the congregation, Solomon my son, whom alone God hath chosen, is yet young and tender, and the work is great: for the palace is not for man, but for the Lord God.

Now I have prepared with all my might for the house of my God the gold for things to made of gold, and the siver for things of silver, and the brass for things of brass, the iron for things of iron, and wood for things of wood; onyx stones, and stones to be set, glistening stones, and of divers colours, and all manner of precious stones, and marble stones in abundance.

Moreover, because I have set my affection to the house of my God, I have of mine own proper good, of gold and silver, which I have given to the house of my God, over and above all that I have prepared for the holy house,

Even three thousand talents of gold, of the gold of Ophir, and seven thousand talents of refined silver, to overlay the walls of the houses withal:

The gold for the things of gold, and the silver for the things of silver, and for all manner of work to be made by the hands of the artificers. And who then is willing to consecrate his service this day unto the Lord?

1 Chronicles 29:1-5

Notice to whom David is talking here — to the whole congregation of the people. He is telling them what he has given and prepared for the building of the temple for the Lord God of Israel. His question to them is: *". . . and who then is willing to consecrate his service this day unto the Lord?"*

When this verse says "service," it is not referring just to manpower, but primarily to gifts, goods, possessions. David wants to know who is going to dedicate his material possessions to the building of the temple.

> Then the chief of the fathers and princes of the tribes of Israel, and the captains of thousands and of hundreds, with the rulers of the king's work, offered willingly.
>
> 1 Chronicles 29:6

How did these people offer their "services"? *Willingly.* Not grudgingly, but willingly. God hates the attitude of a begrudging-type giver. He loves a cheerful giver, one who gives willingly. (2 Cor. 9:7.)

So the people gave willingly for the construction of the temple:

> And gave for the service of the house of God of gold five thousand talents and ten thousand drams, and of silver ten thousand talents, and of brass eighteen thousand talents, and one hundred thousand talents of iron.
>
> And they with whom precious stones were found gave them to the treasure of the house of the Lord, by the hand of Jehiel the Gershonite.
>
> Then the people rejoiced, for that they offered *willingly,* because with perfect heart they offered *willingly* to the Lord: and David the king also rejoiced with great joy.

Wherefore David blessed the Lord before all the congregation: and David said, Blessed be thou, Lord God of Israel our father, for ever and ever.

Thine, O Lord, is the greatness, and the power, and the glory, and the victory, and the majesty: for all that is in the heaven and in the earth is thine; thine is the kingdom, O Lord, and thou art exalted as head above all.

Both riches and honour come of thee, and thou reignest over all; and in thine hand is power and might; and in thine hand it is to make great, and to give strength unto all.

Now therefore our God, we thank thee, and praise thy glorious name.

But who am I, and what is my people, that we should be able to offer so *willingly* after this sort? for all things come of thee, and of thine own have we given thee.

1 Chronicles 9:7-14

So these people gave *willingly* for the work of the Lord. The man of God stood before them and said: "God has given me the plans for the house of the Lord. But I am not the one to build this temple, because I am a man of war. My son, Solomon, will actually be in charge of the construction of the temple. But God has given me the plans. I have willingly laid aside all of these personal possessions which I have brought forth out of my treasury and have dedicated them to the house of the Lord. Now what will you *willingly* give?" And they gave a wealth of material goods!

Here David was asking for financial support. He had given all he had, and he asked the people to also give as he had given. Because they knew that David, their leader, was anointed of God, that God had placed them under his leadership, they too gave generously unto the Lord through David. They wanted to have a share in supporting the man and the work of God. So they went and got their possessions and dedicated them to the Lord. They exhibited an attitude of support.

When you know you're in the place you're supposed to be in, when the man or woman of God stands before you and asks for your support, what should your attitude be? If you *know* that person is God's anointed, then your attitude should be, "I'm going to support this man and this work!"

> Now therefore thus saith the Lord of hosts; Consider your ways.
>
> Ye have sown much, and bring in little; ye eat, but ye have not enough; ye drink, but ye are not filled with drink; ye clothe you, but there is none warm; and he that earneth wages earneth wages to put into a bag with holes.
>
> Haggai 1:5,6

"No matter how much you make," the Lord says to these people in Old Testament days, "it seems like you're just putting it into a bag with holes in it." Why? What was causing these people in the days of Haggai to always be living on a lower level than they should have been financially? What were they doing wrong?

> Thus saith the Lord of hosts; Consider your ways.
>
> Go up to the mountain, and bring wood, and build the house; and I will take pleasure in it, and I will be glorified, saith the Lord.
>
> Ye looked for much, and, lo, it came to little; and when ye brought it home, I did blow upon it. Why? saith the Lord of hosts. Because of mine house that is waste, and ye run every man unto his own house.
>
> Therefore the heaven over you is stayed from dew, and the earth is stayed from her fruit.

> And I called for a drought upon the land, and upon the mountains, and upon the corn, and upon the new wine, and upon the oil, and upon that which the ground bringeth forth, and upon men, and upon cattle, and upon all the labour of the hands.
>
> Then Zerubbabel the son of Shealtiel, and Joshua the son of Josedech, the high priest, with all the remnant of the people, obeyed the voice of the Lord their God, and the words of Haggai the prophet, as the Lord their God had sent him, and the people did fear before the Lord.
>
> Haggai 1:7-12

Who did the people obey? They obeyed the voice of the Lord. What was the Lord telling them to do? He was saying to them:

"Listen My people, you're wondering why things are not going right for you, why you can never make ends meet, why no matter how much you harvest you never have enough. It's because you put yourselves before Me. You put your own priorities before the priorities of Almighty God. You've become selfish and lustful. You just want to satisfy your own selves and to make your own lives comfortable. You've left off building My house in order to construct elegant palaces for yourselves. You have put off construction of the house of the Lord year after year while you have heaped up more and more possessions for yourselves.

"So I have shut up the heavens. You're not going to be blessed any more. Nobody is going to give into your bosom. The windows of heaven are not going to be opened until you build the house of the Lord your God. Until you put the things of God first in your life, until you learn to *support* My work with a willing heart, you won't be blessed the way you should be."

It is time the Body of Christ learned to "hook in" to some ministry and to support that work and that man or woman of God one hundred percent in order to see that vision come to pass.

7
Support — Prayer

Another part of the support that is owed the spiritual leader is prayer support. Every spiritual leader needs the prayers of the people, because more pressure comes against the spiritual leader than against those who follow his leadership. It doesn't matter whether the people in my congregation like me or not, as their pastor I need for them to pray for me.

Some people have asked me, "Pastor Gool, how do you deal with the pressures of life? We have you to counsel with, but who do *you* talk to?"

Jesus. Until there is another brother in the ministry in whom I can confide, I confide only in the Lord. Because, you see, sheep cannot totally and thoroughly understand the leader. Sheep are not in his shoes. They don't have the same assignment and responsibility he bears. Only a fellow minister can know what another minister is experiencing.

So I need the prayers of my people. You need to pray for *your* leader. God doesn't just automatically do things for him just because he's the spiritual leader; he has to use his faith just as you do. He has to believe God as you do. He has to walk in love, to minister to his family, to meet his personal obligations just as you do. Yet he has the added responsibility of the people of his church or ministry. They are his responsibility because God has set him in that particular fellowship as overseer.

Now a member of the congregation may have three or four people in his household to care for. A pastor has his own household, plus three, four, or five hundred — perhaps three, four, or five thousand — others to care for. He needs prayer.

I wonder sometimes how many Christians spend even five minutes a day, every day, praying for their spiritual leader and his or her spouse and family. If every church member prayed one minute a day for their pastor and his family, there is no telling how much more powerful that man of God would be — to say nothing of that church! I wonder how much more would get done if the people truly devoted even five minutes a day to prayer for their leader. I also wonder how much more in tune with God and with his people that leader would become.

So many times we begin our day just praying for *self:* "Lord, bless *me* today. Lord, bless *my* family, *my* home, *my* job, *my* possessions."

Then we "confess the Word of God" upon *ourselves:* "I say that *I* am blessed going in and *I* am blessed going out. Because *I* give, men give generously into *my* bosom. *I* am the head and not the tail, above only and not beneath. No weapon formed against *me* shall prosper, and every tongue that rises up against *me I* condemn in Jesus' name. *I* . . . *me* . . . *my* . . . ." What about the pastor? What about the vision? What about the brothers and sisters in Christ?

Instead, we ought to begin each new day by focusing our minds and hearts on the Lord and His will. God instructs us to pray: first of all for those in positions of authority, the leaders in this country *and* in the Body of Christ — the *whole* Body of Christ, not just our particular segment of it.

Then we need to pray for our Christian family. We should make positive confessions about our brothers and sisters in Christ. A good example would be:

"Father, I confess today that my brothers and sisters in the Body of Christ are the head and not the tail, that they are above only and not beneath, that they have favor with God and man. I confess that their marriages are getting stronger and stronger, their personal and family relationships are being strengthened and enriched day by day. I confess that all their needs are met by Your riches in glory by Christ Jesus."

Finally — lastly — we can pray for ourselves. That's the way to follow the biblical order.

Finally, brethren, pray for us, that the word of the Lord may have free course, and be glorified, even as it is with you.

2 Thessalonians 3:1

So the Apostle Paul, one of the ministry gifts to the Church of his day, asked them to pray for him and his co-workers. He knew they needed that prayer support to carry the Word of God to others.

And that we may be delivered from unreasonable and wicked men: for all men have not faith.

2 Thessalonians 3:2

Paul also knew that he and his co-laborers needed prayer support to resist the attacks that would come their way from those who opposed them and their message.

All the ministry gifts need your prayers. My wife and I, as spiritual leaders, need the prayer support of our people. In fact, that's the thing we want most in life. We want our people to spend time praying for us — praying that our steps will be ordered of the Lord;

that we will be able to preach the Word of the Lord with more accuracy and clarity, with more of an anointing. We want them praying that the wisdom of God will come forth in our lives in a greater way and that we will be an example to the sheep. Also we need intercession that those who are out to get us will not succeed in their plans, that those who speak against our ministry will not be able to overcome us and stop us, and that we won't become discouraged and give up.

That is what Paul was asking these people to pray for him and his team. Paul, one of the greatest apostles who ever lived, asked for prayer. If he needed prayer support, surely those of us in spiritual leadership today need prayer. Paul asked for prayer that the Word would not be hindered from going forth, that those who do not believe would not be able to stop the spreading of the Gospel. Your pastor needs your prayers for the same reason that Paul did.

The Amplified Bible version of this verse reads:

> **Furthermore, brethren, do pray for us, that the Word of the Lord may speed on (spread rapidly and run its course) and be glorified (extolled) and triumph, even as [it has done] with you.**

Do you want the same Word of the Lord that came to you to "speed on," to "spread rapidly and run its course," and "be glorified" and to "triumph"? Do you want to see more and more people receive that Word? In order for that to happen, the Body of Christ must intercede and pray. Prayer is the foundation of every Christian endeavor. We must pray for the leaders, the men and women of God, who are called upon to take the Word to the far corners of this world. Why is prayer necessary? Because God uses our faith-filled prayers to get people into certain positions to hear the Word and to submit to it. If we will dedicate ourselves to prayer, God will see to it that His Word is "speeded on" and "spread rapidly" throughout the earth. That is His will!

If more prayers went up for those in spiritual authority, there is no telling what might be the outcome in terms of souls saved, bodies healed and filled with the Holy Spirit, lives redeemed, marriages restored, families reunited, and homes blessed.

As you read these pages, no doubt you have experienced personally what the Word of the Lord can do in the life of an individual, a marriage, or a family. You have doubtless seen it glorified and triumphant in your own life. You have acted on the Word of God and seen the results it produces when believed and acted on. That is wonderful. That's marvelous. You are very fortunate, greatly blessed.

Guess what? There are others who have not yet heard what you've heard, seen what you've seen, experienced what you've experienced. There are multiplied millions who are still living in bondage, in darkness, in sin. They don't know that they are the righteousness of God in Christ. Some people don't know yet that they have world-overcoming faith resident within them. Paul prayed that the Word of the Lord might be glorified and triumph in the lives of others, even as it was in the lives of those to whom he was writing.

Then in *The Amplified Bible* translation of 2 Thessalonians 3:2, Paul asked that prayer be made:

> . . . that we may be delivered from perverse (improper, unrighteous) and wicked (actively

malicious) men, for not everybody has faith and is held by it.

There are many people in this world who are out to oppose the Gospel and to persecute those who spread it. In fact, I believe that's what Paul's famous "thorn in the flesh" was — opposition and persecution because of his ministry. We need to pray that the ministry gifts will be able to function freely. Whether you realize it or not, those in the ministry receive far more persecution than their followers (laymen). They have the responsibility of ministering the Word of God and the devil doesn't want it preached. They have an anointing that accompanies the office they fill. The enemy will do anything to cause that anointing to become ineffective. He will attack God's ministers in their minds and bodies and homes. He will sow discord and strife in their congregations. He will stir up animosity and provoke church splits. That's why prayer must be constantly wrought for the men and women of God. Because prayer brings deliverance.

You know, sometimes even Christians are used by the adversary to come against spiritual leadership. You and I must pray for our leader that he or she will be delivered from misguided believers. The devil will even use ministers themselves. He will arouse religious jealousy in an attempt to destroy God's anointed. He'll use pride to cause him to begin to accuse other ministries of not preaching the Word as they should or of "ripping off" the people. He'll use prejudice to cause the minister to label other ministries and teachings "of the devil."

Paul knew all of this. That's why he asked his people to pray that he and his teammates would be delivered from ungodly men — and even from those in the Church who would stir up trouble and dissension among the brethren.

We are not just to pray for our spiritual leaders. Nor are we just to pray for our political leaders — the President, the governor, the mayor, the city council. We are to pray for *all* those in positions of authority over us, for *all* those who carry forth the Word of God. We are to pray for Billy Graham, Oral Roberts, Jim Bakker, Pat Robertson, Jerry Falwell, Kenneth Hagin, Kenneth Copeland, Fred Price, Vicki Jamison Peterson, Charles Capps, Jerry Savelle, Marilyn Hickey and many others. Pray for the pastors of the other churches in our city, for all of God's servants, regardless of their church affiliation.

There are enough people out to destroy God's ministers — let's covenant to be among those who are determined to be daily engaged in intercessory prayer for *all* of those who labor in His harvest fields.

Paul says to pray that the Word of the Lord may have free course. That it won't be hindered. I want God's Word to go forth as never before in my hometown of Charlotte, North Carolina. Guess what will cause that to happen? Intercessory prayer for the spiritual leadership in that city. If we are faithful to pray, God will expand the ministries of those who are doing His will. If there are those who are not pleasing to the Lord and are not willing to change, then He will cause them to be removed from their positions of leadership. However, all those who are on fire for the Lord and preaching His Word will be caused to increase and expand by the power of prayer on their behalf.

God wants *your* city. Do your part in helping Him to take it, by giving your prayer support to those whom

He has set in positions of spiritual leadership and authority.

> **Masters, give unto your servants that which is just and equal; knowing that ye also have a Master in heaven.**
>
> **Continue in prayer, and watch in the same with thanksgiving;**
>
> **Withal praying also for us, that God would open unto us a door of utterance, to speak the mystery of Christ, for which I am also in bonds:**
>
> **That I may make it manifest, as I ought to speak.**
>
> **Colossians 4:1-4**

Here Paul writes to the believers in the Colossian church asking them to pray that God will open up doors of ministry to him and his teammates. He also requests that they pray that he will be able to speak as he should — boldly, confidently, accurately, and with an anointing.

Do you want to see more of an anointing on your pastor? *Pray.* Do you want to see more of an anointing on his ministry? *Pray.* Do you want to see more of the things of God in his ministry? *PRAY.* Your prayers will have a great effect on your spiritual leader. Of course, his or her own spiritual relationship with the Lord is involved; but you can have much more of a positive effect that you will ever know. *Your* prayers can make the difference!

Paul says to pray for the ministry gifts. We are to pray for our leader. We must stop talking against him and start praying for him. We must stop turning people against our leader and start lifting him up in intercessory prayer. If you think that your pastor has something to offer humanity, then pray that doors of ministry will be opened to him.

There have been times when members of my congregation have come up to me after a service and told me, "Pastor, I want to help you get that message you shared with us today out to the whole Church of Jesus Christ so many others can be blessed as I was." That is exactly what Paul is talking about here. He says to help our leaders get the Word of the Lord to those in the world who need it most, those who haven't yet heard. He urges us to pray for opportunities of ministry for our spirtual leaders, that doors of opportunity will be opened to them.

Then he also urges that we pray that the leader will make that Word manifest as he should. That he will speak the Word of the Lord as he ought to speak it. We are not to pray that the pastor will say what he thinks is best or what he feels will be most effective, but what the Lord wants Him to say. Pray that he will speak the mind of Christ to the people. Every day, every week, you ought to be praying for your leader that he will get behind the pulpit on Sunday morning, Sunday evening, and other days and say exactly what the Lord has laid on his heart to say.

Our prayer ought to be: "Lord, You know what we need to hear. Give our pastor just the right words to speak to us. Help him to bring forth exactly what we need to hear at this time in our lives, the things that will build our faith and get rid of any mountain of discouragment."

We *must* pray. Paul tells us to pray that God will open up doors of utterance, that those in spiritual leadership may be able to make the Word of the Lord manifest as they should. As Christians, as members of the Body of Christ, that is part of our job — to be intercessors for those in the ministry.

The Apostle Paul said to pray for the ministry gifts. If there is anyone that the devil wants to stop, it is those who have been called into the ministry. He will try anything to defeat them. That's why they need our prayers — because they must face so many trials and so much opposition from the adversary.

I am in the ministry, and I take my wife with me on almost every trip I take. Do you know why I do that? Because I have learned that the devil will have some woman out there who will try to tempt me into sin. But when the devil sees my wife with me, then he knows that he has no chance of leading me off into sin.

The Bible tells us that we must not be ignorant of the enemy's devices. He will use anything to defeat the man of God. You have probably heard of incidents in which some minister of the Lord was tripped up and led into sin by the charms of an attractive woman, or the lure of personal glory, or the deceitfulness of riches. That is another reason we need to pray for our spiritual leaders, so they will be protected against the wiles of the devil.

On Sunday, instead of just getting up late and hurrying down to church, we need to get up early and take time to pray that the gifts of the Spirit will flow as God wills, that sickness will be taken from the midst of His people, that everyone in the service will be blessed and enriched. It won't always be easy getting up early. However, we must *make* time to PRAY!

Many times we come into the church sanctuary and all we do is talk, talk, talk — right up until the service begins. It would be great to come in with a spirit of praise, worship, and prayer! To arrive in the service in a spirit of reverence, a spirit of expectancy, a spirit of participation. To come in praying in tongues, singing in the Spirit. Do you want to see God move in your church services? Then do your part. God will move if you and I will pray and ask Him to do so.

> Now I beseech you, brethren, for the Lord Jesus Christ's sake, and for the love of the Spirit, that ye strive together with me in your prayers to God for me.
>
> Romans 15:30

Notice that Paul requests the Roman Christians to *strive together* with him in their prayers. In other words, Paul is saying: "I myself am praying for the ministry and for the people whom it will reach. Now I want you to join with me in that prayer. Let's *strive* together in prayer. Let's break through in the spirit realm. Let's intercede and pull down Satan's strongholds together."

I wonder if your pastor is the only one praying concerning the vision the Lord has given him. I wonder if you are praying for the ministry God has led you to support. Are you daily *striving* in prayer with your spiritual leader concerning his ministry to your city and area? Remember, we wrestle not against flesh and blood, but against principalities and powers, against the rulers of the darkness of this world, against spiritual wickedness in high (or heavenly) places. And we do it in the Spirit.

The devil doesn't want to see any ministry go any place. He wants to oppose and defeat every ministry aimed against his kingdom. So let's strive together against him in the Spirit. When we do that, there is nothing he can do to stop the advance of the Gospel. Our weapons of warfare are not carnal, but they are mighty through God to the pulling down of demonic strongholds. One of those spiritual weapons is PRAYER!

> That I may be delivered from them that do not believe in Judaea; and that my service which I have for Jerusalem may be accepted of the saints;
>
> That I may come unto you with joy by the will of God, and may with you be refreshed.
>
> **Romans 15:31,32**

Paul asks the Roman believers to pray that he may be able to come to them with joy. Every man of God ought to step into the pulpit with joy, because he's heard from God, because he has a message for the people, because he's been blessed and fired up. He shouldn't have to come in saying, "Oh, boy, it's been such a hard week, and now I've got to get up there behind that pulpit and preach!" No, he should come with joy, because his people have been praying for him and he has heard from God.

We are talking about an attitude of prayer support. If you believe you are where God wants you to be, then you ought to be praying for your spiritual leader. It stands to reason that if you support a minister with your finances, you would be supporting him with your prayers.

> And many of the brethren in the Lord, waxing confident by my bonds, are much more bold to speak the word without fear.
>
> Some indeed preach Christ even of envy and strife; and some also of good will:
>
> The one preach Christ of contention, not sincerely, supposing to add affliction to my bonds:
>
> But the other of love, knowing that I am set for the defence of the gospel.

What then? notwithstanding, every way, whether in pretence, or in truth, Christ is preached; and I therefore do rejoice, yea, and will rejoice.

Philippians 1:14-18

Here Paul says that some people are preaching Christ because of strife, simply to make Paul mad or jealous. But his reaction is: "I don't care whether they are preaching in an effort to irritate me or whether they are preaching out of a heart of love; all I care about is the fact that Christ — the Living Word of God — is being preached. That's what matters. And because He is being preached — for whatever reason — I rejoice and will continue to rejoice."

Why? Why is Paul rejoicing even when in prison, even when his detractors and enemies are attempting to belittle and harrass him by preaching Christ in his absence?

For I know that this shall turn to my salvation *through your prayers* and the supply of the Spirit of Jesus Christ.

Philippians 1:19

Paul rejoices because he knows that his deliverance is on the way — *through the prayers of his people.* Paul was confident that the prayers of the people of Philippi would cause the Spirit of God to move, an anointing to be made manifest, and a deliverance to come to pass. When the people prayed, Paul expected something to happen.

The Amplified Bible version of this scripture reads:

Yes, and I shall rejoice [hereafter] also. For I am well assured and indeed know that through your prayers and a bountiful supply of the Spirit of Jesus Christ, the Messiah, this will turn out for my preservation [for the spiritual health and welfare of my own soul and avail toward the saving work of the Gospel].

109

That's what prayer for your spiritual leader does. It brings a bountiful supply of the Spirit to work on his behalf. Make sure that you pray daily for the ministry gifts, for the vision of your church, for the ministry you support, for your city, state, and world. Pray that the Lordship of Jesus Christ will be made manifest in them all. Give your leadership your prayer support. It is powerful!

8
Support — Physical

Then came Amalek, and fought with Israel in Rephidim.

And Moses said unto Joshua, Choose us out men, and go out, fight with Amalek: to morrow I will stand on the top of the hill with the rod of God in mine hand.

So Joshua did as Moses had said to him, and fought with Amalek: and Moses, Aaron, and Hur went up to the top of the hill.

And it came to pass, when Moses held up his hand, that Israel prevailed: and when he let down his hand, Amalek prevailed.

But Moses' hands were heavy; and they took a stone, and put it under him, and he sat thereon; and Aaron and Hur stayed up his hands, the one on the one side, and the other on the other side; and his hands were steady until the going down of the sun.

And Joshua discomfited Amalek and his people with the edge of the sword.

Exodus 17:8-13

So the Israelites went to battle with the people of Amalek. Obviously, Moses had received instructions from the Lord on how to wage this warfare because he went to the top of the hill to oversee the battle. At the summit of the hill, Moses raised his hands. As long as his hands were up in the air, the Israelites would push their enemies back. But when his arms would get tired and his hands begin to come down, then the Amaleks would begin to take the field.

Have you ever been in a church service in which the leader asked everyone to stretch out their hands toward one particular person in intercessory prayer for him or her? Have you ever stretched out your arm toward someone and then had to hold it there while the leader talked or prayed for five minutes or more? What happened? Didn't your arm begin to get tired and your hand begin to droop? That's what happened to Moses here. His arms began to get heavy, so he found it hard to keep them raised in the air. Every time his hands went down, the Israelites would start to lose. What could he do? What was the answer to his problem? *Physical support.*

Seeing the situation, Aaron and Hur ran up to Moses and told him, "Moses, we see what needs to be done here. Sit down on this stone, and we will stand on either side of you and hold up your hands for you. That way, our troops will continue to win the battle."

Now notice that Aaron and Hur did NOT say, "Hey, look! Moses is getting tired. This is our chance to take over!" Instead, they came and supported him. They lifted up his tired arms and bolstered his waning strength.

As a pastor, I want you to know that your spiritual leader needs that very same type support from his people. There is no man or woman of God who can do it all alone. There comes a time in the life of every minister when he needs somebody who will come and stand beside him — physically, tangibly — and help him hold his hand to the plow. Not someone who will try to take advantage of the situation and put himself in control, but someone who will support the one God has set in the position of leadership.

Many times when people see the man of God becoming weary, they want to jump up and take over instead of going to him and saying, "Can I help you; I'm available, what can I do?" We need to learn to flow with the plan of God.

Aaron and Hur didn't try to take over. They simply held up Moses' hands, one on one side and one on the other. That is a good example to the Church today. It is high time the Body of Christ quit trying to become leaders and learn first to be good followers. It's time we quit looking for "positions" and just made ourselves available for service. Christians need to make their talents, skills and know-how available to their ministers. Not just verbally either. Every time an opportunity for service arises, Christians ought to be ready to step in and lend a hand as Aaron and Hur did for Moses.

The problem is that many times people make themselves available with their mouths. When the time for actual work comes, they always seem to have excuses. They've got to do this, or that, or the other. It's always a "bad time" for them. They have something else that must be done first. The Lord said for us to give *first* place to His kingdom and His righteousness. We must learn to set our affections on things above, not on things here below.

> And it came to pass on the morrow, that Moses sat to judge the people: and the people stood by Moses from the morning unto the evening.
>
> And when Moses' father in law saw all that he did to the people, he said, What is this thing that thou doest to the people? why sittest thou thyself *alone*, and all the people stand by thee from morning unto even?
>
> And Moses said unto his father in law, Because the people come unto me to inquire of God:

When they have a matter, they come unto me; and I judge between one and another, and I do make them know the statutes of God, and his laws.

And Moses' father in law said unto him, The thing that thou doest is not good.

Thou wilt surely wear away, both thou, and this people that is with thee: for this thing is too heavy for thee; thou art not able to perform it thyself *alone*.

Exodus 18:13-18

Any man of God who thinks he can do it all by himself is mistaken. If he endeavors to do it all alone, he will eventually wear himself out.

When my wife and I began our current ministry, Victory Christian Center, we believed God for the ministry of helps to accompany it. We prayed and released our faith that God would send us the right people to help us. We decided that until those people were sent to us, we would do what we knew to do ourselves. We did the necessary work and the Lord honored our faith. He began to send us the workers we needed. He is still sending people to take part in the ministry He has given us.

We believe that the Lord adds to His Church daily. But our faith is also out that He will add the specific ones to our particular ministry that really should be involved in it. We believe that the Lord is adding to our church the specific persons who belong in it, those ordained by God to be an Aaron or a Hur. God is adding those people. I believe that there are certain ones whom God has planned to be in the ministry with us for specific reasons. Maybe they are not meant to remain with us forever, but only for a certain season of time in order to accomplish a specific job in the growth of the ministry.

There is not a ministry gift in this country that is able to succeed by himself; every ministry gift must believe God for those who will become partners with them and help carry out God's plan for their lives.

A word of warning here: a lot of men of God have made a mistake by setting just anybody in a position of responsibility in the church. Then they have hell on earth because they were not careful whom they set on the deacon board, the board of stewards, the panel of ushers, or the Sunday School faculty. They put people in the choir who can't carry a note in a bucket, or people who can sing but are show-offs and not ready for ministry. They place people on administrative boards who are totally incapable of handling serious church matters. Many times they choose deacons or elders simply because they have a business degree or are in business for themselves. The thought is, if such people are capable of running their own business, then they can run the business of the church. That is not always the case. The best qualified candidate is not always the candidate the world would pick; it's the one whom God has chosen — the one in whom He has put His mind and heart.

As a spiritual leader, you have to believe God for your Aarons, your Hurs, and your Joshuas. You can't place just anybody in a position in the church.

I remember a dear friend of mine who did that very thing. My wife and I counseled with him and tried to warn him that he had to be careful whom he chose to fill positions of responsibility in his church. However, he didn't listen to us. He went right ahead and named unprepared persons to major positions. Eventually that church crumbled. Every ministry must walk in wisdom and believe God to supply those best qualified for positions of honor and responsibility.

It doesn't matter if a person has a doctorate in music, he or she is not necessarily the best qualified to lead the choir. In fact, the best person for that job may not be able to read a note of music. Ministry gifts have to follow the Spirit because it is He Who leads them to the church for His purpose. It is God Who places the anointing upon them to do what He has called and set them aside to do.

In choosing leaders, in making decisions, we must be careful to seek the Lord's will. The Bible tells us:

Trust in the Lord with all thine heart; lean not unto thine own understanding.

In all thy ways acknowledge him, and he shall direct thy paths.

Proverbs 3:5,6

In matters of spiritual service, you can't just trust your own mind and choose the person who *seems* to have the best qualifications on paper. Instead, you must pray and allow the Lord to reveal to you the person He has chosen and anointed, the one He wants in that position. As good as proper qualifications are, it is important to remember that the Bible says: **But God hath chosen the foolish things of the world to confound the wise; and he hath chosen the weak things of the world to confound the things which are mighty** (1 Cor. 1:27). Peter and John were unlearned and ignorant fishermen, but God used them to confound the wisdom of the Saducees and Pharisees. (Acts 4:13.) Never forget, the call and the anointing make all the difference in the world.

This is an area that demands that the Body of Christ walk in love. Although we may be the most qualified for a particular position or job in the church, that does not necessarily mean that we will be asked to fill it. If that happens, we must be willing to walk in love and not get our feelings hurt. We must learn to pray for our leaders and resist the temptation to get into jealousy, envy and strife. We must simply concede that God knows what He's doing — that He's smarter than we are. We must remind ourselves that since we have prayed that our leaders will be led of the Spirit of God, then we must believe that they are being led of Him. We must not give into the temptation to quit the church, start rumors, stir up strife, or cause contention. Instead, we must walk in love, believing that God is still in charge and that He knows what He's doing (even if He hasn't made it clear to us yet what it is). It just may be that He has something else — something better — in mind for us.

Remember that Moses' father-in-law came to him and said, "Moses, why are you doing this? Why are you taking on the burden of judging every one of these people all by yourself. You can't do it. You'll wear yourself out — and them too." Then he suggested a better way for Moses to lead the people and settle their disputes.

> Hearken now unto my voice, I will give thee counsel, and God shall be with thee: Be thou for the people to God-ward, that thou mayst bring the causes unto God:
>
> And thou shalt teach them ordinances and laws, and shalt shew them the way wherein they must walk, and the work that they must do.
>
> Moreover thou shalt provide out of all the people able men, such as fear God, men of truth, hating

**covetousness; and place such over them, to be rulers
of thousands, and rulers of hundreds, rulers of fifties,
and rulers of tens:**

**And let them judge the people at all seasons: and
it shall be, that every great matter they shall bring unto
thee, but every small matter they shall judge: so shall
it be easier for thyself, and *they shall bear the burden
with thee.***

**If thou shalt do this thing, and God command
thee so, then thou shalt be able to endure, and all this
people shall go to their place in peace.**

Exodus 18:19-23

In other words, Moses' father-in-law said, "Moses,
you're wearing yourself out. Choose some men to help
you. If you don't, you're going to kill yourself and wear
the people out as well. But if you do what I suggest
(and if it is in accordance with God's will), then you
and all these people will be blessed."

**So Moses hearkened to the voice of his father in
law, and did all that he had said.**

**And Moses chose able men out of all Israel, and
made them heads over the people, rulers of thousands,
rulers of hundreds, rulers of fifties, and rulers of tens,**

**And they judged the people at all seasons: the
hard causes they brought unto Moses, but every small
matter they judged themselves.**

Exodus 18:24-26

So at Jethro's suggestion, and with the Lord's
approval, Moses chose seventy men to rule the children
of Israel. The Lord told Moses, "I will take of your spirit
and rest it upon them. Then they will be able to serve
in their capacities with an anointing."

When that happened, leading and judging the
great crowd became much easier for Moses and
everything went much smoother for all involved.

Things began to run more like a fine-tuned engine. The only thing that Moses himself had to deal with personally were the weightier matters because those seventy men were anointed to deal with the lighter issues. That's the way the church and ministries must function. The minister cannot deal with every little thing. He needs some physical help, some physical support to deal with the things of lesser importance so he can be freed to handle more pressing matters.

Be open to the Lord and how you can physically support your pastor and other ministry gifts. Maybe you could babysit, wash the car, cut the grass — there are so many ways to be a blessing. Remember, even Jesus needed help.

The spiritual leader needs financial support, because like everyone else in the church he needs to live well. He needs prayer support, because he too has to deal with the problems and affairs of everyday life in addition to his ministry. And he needs physical suppport to free him for those things which are most essential and of primary importance to the welfare of all concerned.

That support must come from those who have committed themselves to share as partners with their spiritual leader in the ministry to which the Lord has called him.

9
Every Part You Play Is Important

You may have heard of Willie George Ministries. It's my understanding that Willie George got started in the ministry by cleaning toilets. He accepted that job in the church as a service unto the Lord. From there he was promoted to the job of door greeter or usher. Step by step he was advanced by the Lord until today he has one of the most effective full-time children's ministries in the Body of Christ.

Why did this happen? Why was he promoted and advanced? This happened because he made himself available and worked with all his might. He was willing to go to his pastor and say, "Pastor, do you have anything you need done?" Wherever and whatever the need in the church, Willie George was ready to help. He was available, realizing that every job is important.

As Christians, that's the way all of us ought to be. We ought to be recognized and identified by a love that moves us to want to serve the Body in whatever way we can. Then we ought to work hard at whatever our assigned task is. If our motivation is promotion, then we have the wrong motive. Our heart is not right before the Lord. We need to be willing to flow with the Holy Spirit and to put our hands to anything, allowing the anointing of the Lord to work through us, becoming proficient at our assigned task.

Sometimes as Christians we get too proud. We allow pride to keep us from accepting work which we feel is "beneath our level." That is a wrong attitude. The

Bible warns that pride goes before a fall. (Prov. 16:18.) Remaining humble under the hand of the Lord allowing Him to promote you in His time is a valuable key to success. When Saul was little in his own eyes, God gave him the kingdom. This principle has been a way of life for me.

Soon after I got married, my wife became pregnant. Realizing I had a responsibility to support us, I took a job at McDonald's. I worked hard at it. Dedication was so obvious, the management wanted to send me to college — Hamburger University. Some of my friends, however, were too proud to work in a "hamburger joint."

"You won't see me working at McDonald's," they would say. "Why, I'm a graduate of Oral Roberts University."

Well, so am I. The difference was that I was willing to humble myself and do anything that was honest and clean. I was willing to put my hand to what was available, and work with all my might. I trusted the Lord to promote me, to open doors that no man can close, to give me favor, and He did. When it came time to leave McDonald's, my supervisors wanted to give me another raise — anything to keep me there. I told them that I was called to preach the Gospel so I had to move on.

I didn't work there with a superior attitude. I didn't show up for work with a begrudging attitude, acting as though all this was beneath me. I showed the same attitude at McDonald's that I showed at church or at ORU. I was pleasant and agreeable. I worked as to the Lord. When the time came, the Lord gave me favor and promoted me out of that job to a better job and then to full-time ministry.

For the Lord to promote us, we must be willing to humble ourselves so that He can lift us up. I remember Kenneth Copeland telling about how God promoted him in the ministry. He said that after he was called into the ministry, he went out to Oral Roberts University and while there accepted a job as airplane pilot for Brother Roberts. All he did was fly him from one place to the other, open car doors for him, hold his coat, drive him around town and to the hotel and airport. He was a sort of a valet service to Brother Roberts for a while. He kept his mouth closed and didn't engage Brother Roberts in conversation unless he was asked a question. The reason he did that was because he respected his position and the position that Brother Roberts filled.

In time, the Lord promoted Brother Copeland into his own ministry, and now he has others who serve him just as he used to serve another. That's true ministry.

Now I'm not talking about spending your whole life shining someone else's shoes (unless that's what the Lord wants). I'm talking about the proper attitude we need to have toward those in positions of spiritual leadership. However, there could be times when we may need to shine shoes or wash cars for our leaders. If that's what's needed, then that's what we ought to do. Everybody's part is important.

There have been times since I've been in the ministry when someone in my church has come to me and said, "Pastor Gool, the Lord wants me to shine your shoes for you."

I have always said, "Fine. I'd appreciate that very much. I need it." I have heard other ministers such as

Lester Sumrall say the same thing, that they are so busy in ministry they don't give much attention to those kinds of things. Whenever someone volunteers to do them a personal service, it is received as a gift from the Lord, with humility and gratitude. Sometimes it takes as much humility to *receive* ministry as it does to *give* it.

Every man of God needs for the Body of Christ to be sensitive to the Holy Ghost and to do those things He directs them to do to *help advance* the cause of Christ. If that involves rendering personal favors or services to the spiritual leader, then neither the Body nor the leader should be too proud to allow the Lord to do what needs to be done. *I'm not telling you to do these things for your pastor or leader.* I'm simply saying that there needs to be an attitude of "What can I do to help?" When God's people have that attitude, then the Holy Ghost will start sharing with them what they can and should do. Sometimes that may be simply shining the pastor's shoes or washing his car or doing his laundry or cleaning his house. Who knows? Be available, because everybody has a part to play and every part is important.

None of us should be offended if the Lord directs us to render such service to another person in the Body of Christ. Neither should we be offended if the Lord directs someone else to do us such a favor. When someone offered to shine my shoes for me, I didn't get offended. I didn't say, "Are you telling me that I don't know how to take care of myself? Do you think I need *you* to groom me?" No, I received that offer as from the Lord and was grateful and appreciative.

There have been times when people have offered to wash my car for me. I didn't get offended and think they thought I was too lazy or stupid to do it myself. I accepted their favor as a sign of love and respect and concern. Having those things done for me saves me time. Praise God!

Believers and ministers must be on guard against becoming so "high and mighty" that we can't receive — or give — support to one another. The Body of Christ has to be sensitive to the Holy Ghost relative to the helps ministry. We have to remember that we are all part of each other and of our Lord Jesus Christ.

In 1 Corinthians 12:27, the Apostle Paul reminds us:

Now ye are the body of Christ, and members in particular.

Realize that God doesn't lump all of us together. No, we are members *in particular.* We are each special, unique, and valuable. You are an individual. The Lord has something special for you to do. You are His workmanship, created in Christ Jesus unto good works. (Eph. 2:10.) He has things for you to do that no one else on earth can do quite like you.

And God hath set some in the church, first apostles, secondarily prophets, thirdly teachers, after that miracles, then gifts of healings, helps, govern-ments, diversities of tongues.

1 Corinthians 12:28

Paul tells us that it is God Who has set these different ministries in the Church. They are given to help the Body of Christ, to be a blessing to the Church and the ministry. One way laymen help the Lord's ministry is by helping His chosen leader. But in order to help, we must have the right attitude and make ourselves available to the Lord for His purpose.

And Jesus went about all the cities and villages, teaching in their synagogues, and preaching the gospel of the kingdom, and healing every sickness and every disease among the people.

But when he saw the multitudes, he was moved with compassion on them, because they fainted, and were scattered abroad, as sheep having no shepherd.

Then saith he unto his disciples, The harvest truly is plenteous, but the labourers are few.

Pray ye therefore the Lord of the harvest, that he will send forth labourers into his harvest.

Matthew 9:35-38

When you and I pray that the Lord will send forth laborers into His harvest, we must make ourselves available to be one of those laborers. When you pray for the Lord to send out workers, don't think of someone else. Instead, say, "Lord, send forth laborers into Your harvest. And here am I; send me."

And when he had called unto him his twelve disciples, he gave them power against unclean spirits, to cast them out, and to heal all manner of sickness and all manner of disease.

Matthew 10:1

Notice when Jesus saw the multitudes, He was moved with compassion. When He saw how vast the fields were and how the people were scattered because they had no shepherd, He realized that in order to help them He needed help. He knew that He alone in physical form could never hope to preach and teach and lay hands on all those vast numbers of people.

The Lord needed help then. He needs help now. His call to pray for workers is directed as much to us today as it was to the disciples in their day. We too are disciples. We too are called to *pray* for laborers — and to *be* laborers. He has chosen and commissioned us, just as He chose and commissioned the twelve. Every believer has been sent forth to preach the Gospel, to cast out devils, to heal the sick. He has given us power and authority to do it in His name.

You don't have to stand behind a pulpit to proclaim the Gospel. That can be done on the street corner, in the factory, in the office, in the field, on the campus. Wherever there are people at work and play, there are opportunities to preach and heal and help. Ministry gifts can't get out to all those places and to all those people. However, believers go there every day as part of their daily routine. They *have* to go to the office, the school, the field, the factory. All believers must realize they have a responsibility, a commission, to share the Good News, to lay hands on the sick, and to serve people wherever they go in their daily lives. It's called teamwork.

"But that's what we pay the pastor to do!" many church members are quick to argue.

No, that's not right. That's a wrong attitude toward leadership and Christian service. Jesus saw the multitide and was moved with compassion. He realized that He, the Chief Shepherd, the Pastor, could not get to all the people by Himself. So He turned to His disciples and called them to Himself. He gave them power to go preach, teach and minister to the sick. He commissioned and authorized them to act in His name, in His place.

> These twelve Jesus sent forth, and commanded them, saying . . . .
> . . . as ye go, preach . . . .
> Heal the sick, cleanse the lepers, raise the dead, cast out devils: freely ye have received, freely give.
> Matthew 10:5,7,8

Not only did Jesus send the twelve, but in Luke 10 we find seventy others who were called into the *ministry of helps.* After the resurrection, every believer was enlisted. Our Lord cannot reach the world except through us. We are His hands and feet and voice. He has left us a command to obey and a calling to fulfill.

Friend, if you are a Christian, *you* are called into the ministry of helps. It is your job to support the ministry gifts, to help get the word out, to help get people saved and well and set free from demonic oppression. The power and authority to accomplish the job is there. All that's needed now is for you to accept your calling and begin to fulfill it.

Maintain a proper attitude toward leadership, supporting those in spiritual authority. Get involved in the Lord's work, never despising the nature of it. By doing so, you're supplying your part, your important part, and helping to fulfill the Great Commission.

Let's pray together now concerning this. Let's put our faith together about being a blessing. Pray this out loud this very moment:

"Heavenly Father, in the name of Jesus I come boldly before the throne of grace. I desire to be a blessing to the ministry gift. I join my faith right now with Brother Robyn for You to show me how to help my pastor, how to help ministry gifts.

"I believe now for the insight and direction of the Holy Spirit. As an act of my will, I make myself available to You to be a blessing. I realize that every part is important, and I thank You for my role.

"Heavenly Father, I put You in remembrance of Your Word. In Matthew 10:41,42 You said, **He that**

receiveth a prophet in the name of a prophet shall receive a prophet's reward . . . . and whosoever shall give to drink unto one of these little ones a cup of cold water only in the name of a disciple, . . . he shall in no wise lose his reward. I receive Your ministry gifts to the Church and as I commit myself to being a blessing to them, I thank You for the promised return. I believe that I receive it.

"In Jesus' name, amen."

About Our Tape Ministry

In July of 1980, under the direction of the Holy Spirit, Robyn and Marilyn Gool began Victory Christian Center. The Center is designed to be a church based ministry that teaches believers the principles of the Word of God and trains them to make a positive difference in their communities and the world.

"More Than Conquerors Ministries" is the name of the outreach ministries of VCC, which presently include the spreading of the Gospel through radio and teaching tapes. The tape ministry fulfills one of the objectives of VCC, which is to use the media as a tool to take the Gospel to all people.

The teaching tapes offered by this ministry are produced with quality, and we expect them to bless and minister to all who listen. If any tape you order should be defective in any way, please return it within 90 days for replacement.

Cassette Tape List

Healing Series — $32.75

RG 317 God's Perspective On Healing.........................No. 1
RG 318 God's Perspective On Healing.........................No. 2
RG 319 God's Perspective On Healing.........................No. 3
RG 320 God's Perspective On Healing.........................No. 4
RG 321 God's Perspective On Healing.........................No. 5
RG 322 God's Perspective On Healing.........................No. 6
RG 323 God's Perspective On Healing.........................No. 7
RG 324 God's Perspective On Healing.........................No. 8
RG 325 God's Perspective On Healing.........................No. 9

Consecration & Dedication Series — $11.75

RG 586 God Desires To Be Our Only God..................No. 1
RG 587 Choosing God's Way ....No. 2
RG 589 To What Extreme Will You Go ....No. 3

Success Series I — $15.25

RG 374 Humility — A Key To Success ....No. 1
RG 517 Change A Losing Game................................No. 2

Singles Series

Marriage Series

Single Tapes — $4.00 Each

RG 555 God Will Exalt You
RG 556 What Will This Man Do? — What Is That To You?
RG 557 The Power Of Unity
RG 558 Together, On One Accord — For The City
RG 559 How Do You See Things
RG 560 The True Spirit Of Christmas
RG 561 Where Are You Going In Life?
RG 562 Be Not Envious Of Evildoers
RG 563 If You Can Believe
RG 564 You Are The Light Of The World
RG 565 Everything Can Change With God
RG 566 Fear
RG 567 Sex Before Marriage — Why Not?
RG 568 Being A Believer
RG 569 What To Do Between The Sowing And Reaping
RG 570 Six Prerequisites To Answered Prayer
RG 571 We're All One In Christ
RG 572 Judge Ye Not
RG 573 Rebellion
RG 574 What Manner Of Child Shall This Be?
RG 575 Being A Doer Of The Word
RG 576 Remember The Lessons That You've Learned
RG 577 Resist Doubt
RG 578 Everything God Has Is For You — I
RG 579 Everything God Has Is For You — II
RG 580 The Love Of God — I
RG 581 The Love Of God — II
RG 582 The Importance Of The Word — I
RG 583 The Importance Of The Word — II
RG 584 The Pre-Adamic Race — I
RG 585 The Pre-Adamic Race — II

Tapes By Marilyn Gool

$19.00 Per Set
CHRISTIAN GROWTH
MG 090 Commitment & Growth.................................No. 1
MG 091 Commitment & Growth.................................No. 2
MG 092 Commitment & Growth.................................No. 3

Single Tapes — $4.00 Each

MG 097 God's Pattern For Praise & Worship
MG 098 Why We Praise & Worship The Way We Do
MG 223 Woman — Full Of The Word — Full Of Joy
MG 225 The Grace Of God
MG 239 Jesus Loves The Little Children — What About You?
Part I
MG 240 Jesus Loves The Little Children — What About You?
Part II
MG 246 Come See A Man — Part 1
MG 247 Come See A Man — Part 2
MG 248 Circumstances
MG 249 Have Confidence In God
MG 250 God And The Married Woman
MG 251 God's Single Lady
MG 252 Woman! You Have Power With God
MG 253 Even Though I Was Displeased, I Never Gave Up On You
MG 254 Homework Assignment — Love Indeed
MG 255 Organization In The Home
MG 256 Jesus, The Christ — The Messiah Of God

Send Order To:
(Please Print Clearly)
Name: _____
Address: _____
City: _____ State: _____
Zip: _____

Tape No.	Quantity	Amount
	Tax 4½%	
	Total	

Mail To:
M.T.C.M.
P.O. Box 5301
Charlotte, NC 28225-5301

Pastor Robyn Gool

is also author of

For Singles Only

This is a book that you will want to read whether you are a parent, a teacher, or someone connected in any way with the world of the single person.

It contains timely advice for the Christian single in today's society. Preparatory tips for the physical, mental, financial and spiritual facets of life are presented, plus spiritual counsel for the unique problems and opportunities which face unmarried believers everywhere.

For Singles Only
You don't want to miss it!

NOTES

NOTES

NOTES